Paratrooper To Preacher

John Lee

Dr. Mike Tapia

ISBN-13: 978-1717025609

Dedication

This book is dedicated to all those ordinary men and women who have given their lives in the service of our ruler, King Jesus, selflessly giving of themselves and their resources to further the cause of Christ. They are the true heroes of the Faith. In addition, we would like to dedicate and give honor to those brave men and women who have lived and died serving our great country. Because of their sacrifice, the Gospel can freely be proclaimed.

CONTENTS

Acknowledgments

I would like to thank my Lord and Savior Jesus Christ for allowing me to be used by Him for His purposes, and for giving me the strength to write my testimony. I would also like to thank my beautiful wife Kelly who has been at my side through all the Joys and trials over the years. Without her support, I would not be the man God intended me to be. To my brave and loving children John, Matt, and Teresa who have loved and supported me and whom God used to inspire me to keep moving forward regardless of the circumstances. I would also like to acknowledge my co-author and mentor Pastor Mike for his God-given wisdom and encouragement through the last several years. I would be remiss if I did not thank the men of the 173rd 1/503 M.O.D Company for their strength and encouragement during our time in Afghanistan.

Paratrooper To Preacher

Introduction

Have you ever heard the phrase, "God uses ordinary people to accomplish extraordinary things"? Well it is true. Throughout the history of humanity, God chose ordinary people to fulfill His extraordinary plans. Just think of God's call to Abraham in Genesis chapter 12.

"Now the Lord said to Abram: Get out of your country, from your family and from your father's house, to a land that I will show you."

Abraham obeyed and the rest is *His*-tory. Now try not to miss this, Abraham was just an ordinary man but he was serving an extraordinary God. As we follow and obey Him, he gives each of us a testimony. The Hebrew word is *eduwth,* which is translated as evidence or witness. It first appears in the scriptures in Exodus 16:34, referring to when God fed His people in the wilderness. Exodus 16:33-35 says, "And Moses said to Aaron, 'Take a pot and put an omer of manna in it, and lay it up before the Lord, to be kept for your generations.' As the Lord commanded Moses, so Aaron laid it up before the Testimony, to be kept. And the children of Israel ate manna forty years, until they came to an inhabited land; they ate manna until they came to the border of the land of Canaan."

God not only wanted them to remember, but that a witness be established for future generations. This Testimony would later be placed in the Ark of the Covenant or Ark of the Testimony once it was built. You see, God wanted this Testimony to point to Him, not only for Israel's sake, but for the sake of all humanity.

Inside the Ark of the Testimony, God had them place the two tablets of the Law, Aaron's rod and the jar of manna. Each of these items was a symbol of God's great love and power to both His people and those around them. The two tablets were engraved with God's covenant with His people that provided a way for an unholy people to be in a relationship with a Holy God. Aaron's rod was instrumental in the release of God's people from the oppressive hands of Pharaoh. The rod would serve as a reminder that He was their God and delivered them from captivity and oppression. Finally, the manna represented God's provision and care for them. He was not only their God, He was their Father who knew their needs and was more than able to sustain and care for them in the wilderness.

In like manner, God gives each of His people a Testimony, not only as a remembrance of His goodness, but also as a witness of His grace and mercy. In Romans 10:17 we read, "so then faith comes by hearing, and hearing by the word of God." As we hear God's word it provides us with the avenue to be in a right relationship with Him. "The Word became flesh and dwelt among us and we beheld His glory, the glory as of the only begotten of the

Father, full of grace and truth" (John 1:14). Through His word, He reveals to us His plan of salvation. Through His word He unlocks our understanding of His purposes and plans as He guides and directs us through this life. The fact that we even have a Testimony is due to the power of His Word.

Aaron's rod was a symbol of God's power to release His people from captivity and to lead them on to freedom. After salvation, your testimony is a reminder that God is still in the business of releasing the captives--not from slavery in Egypt but from bondage to sin itself. The Testimony of a changed life cannot be underestimated.

Much like the *omer* was to be placed in the Ark of the Testimony as a witness to God's provision and goodness as He cared for His people for 40 years in the wilderness, God's mercy and grace in our lives serves as a testimony to those around us. Your personal Testimony is one of the most powerful tools you have to help others come to the knowledge of God, and not only that, it becomes an anchor for your life as you encounter stormy waters.

So it's true, God uses ordinary people to accomplish extraordinary things. As you read through the pages of this book, be encouraged not just in the fact that can He use you, but that He desires to use you to accomplish great and mighty things as you submit yourself to His Lordship and His will.

Chapter 1

"You remind us of Job"

April through August of 2008 were months to remember. God had started stripping me of all the things, situations, and pre-conceived notions that were impeding me from doing His work. He was also refining and teaching me that I was created for His works, which were to be done on *His* terms. I was a relatively new Christian, and I aspired to go to Seminary, preach the Word, and pastor a church. I had life all planned out, or so I thought.

Shortly after becoming a Christian, I started a business that I felt was doing well. I had taken my first major step of faith by quitting my job while trying to support my wife and three kids. I was feeling pretty good about myself and my leap of faith. I started the business in 2005 with a man I met while working at a previous company. I remember the day I walked into my job and told them out of the blue that I was leaving. They were quite baffled by my sudden decision and asked, "How are you going to support your family?" and "Didn't you just buy a new house?"

I proudly told them I would rather go broke than work there any longer because I did not agree with their business practices, and besides that, I had faith that God would take care my family and me. Well one thing was for sure, God *would* take care of us, but it certainly would not be in the way I imagined, or even when I thought it would be.

When I was 9 years old I was sitting at a Christmas Eve service with my mom and dad. I suddenly sensed warmth, purpose and an overwhelming feeling that someday I wanted to talk about God like the priest up front did. What I did not know was that God was beginning to draw me to Himself and the seeds of His purpose for my life were planted within me. The strange feeling I felt that day would never leave me.

I would not say I was a Christian at the time. I went to church because I was told to go by my parents. We went mostly on Christmas and Easter, but regardless I always carried this urge to know more about what this God and Jesus thing was all about. It would be several years before my walk with Christ would start and those seeds of purpose began to grow.

My new wife and I bought our first house in 2001. We were greeted by these really nice neighbors two houses down from us who were so welcoming. They would stop by just to chat, and soon after we moved in they began inviting us to church. They were not pushy about it, just persistent and open about their faith. I would often talk with my neighbor about the things of God for hours while standing in my driveway. While I appreciated his point of view, I was convinced the Jesus thing was not for me. My wife decided to take them up on their invitation and started attending church on a regular basis with the kids . I thought that was great for her and our kids, but I had my own relationship with God and didn't need to go to a building to experience Him. After all, I could do that anywhere. I was pretty hard-hearted when it came to the whole church and Jesus thing because I felt it only caused division and was too confusing.

A few months went by. It was on a Sunday, so I knew my wife was at her new church with the kids. As I sat home bored and lonely, I thought to myself, *I'm going to stop in and support her and the kids in their new venture.* As I walked into the service I was greeted by just about everyone there and they all had smiles on their faces. They seemed friendly enough and this certainly was not how I remembered church being as a kid. When the service began there was a band on the stage playing what sounded to me at the time like rock n roll hymns, which I thought was pretty cool considering I was brought up Catholic with a formal service. It was not until I heard the preacher that my eyes and heart were opened. He was preaching from the Gospel of Matthew and it was at that point that God grabbed me tight and would not let me go. I began attending on a regular basis to check out this Jesus Church thing. It would take me several months before I would confess my faith in Jesus Christ, but He had me right where He wanted me and was not letting me go.

I should have known at the beginning of my walk that my plans for my life were not the same as God's. My desire to preach grew stronger and stronger as I sat in the pews week after week. I would often have that same feeling I had when I was 9 years old. I wanted to talk about God like the guy up front did. I was convinced that because of my extensive construction background I would sign up for the maintenance team at the church. It seemed like the perfect fit for me. I never heard back from the team, but as God would have it, I was asked to teach the Junior High Sunday school class because the current teacher recently left the church. At first I was taken aback, but reluctantly agreed and so began the unfolding of God's plan and purpose.

This all happened around the same time I started my business My desire to preach kept growing stronger the more I served and attended the church. My master plan was to start a business, go to seminary, fund mission trips, become a pastor, and make a lot of money. To me this sounded like a great plan! I would get what I wanted and God would get what He wanted. It was a win-win as far as I was concerned. After all, I was doing it for God, so surely He would bless me and my family, and I would prosper and do mighty things. Well, God definitely blessed my family, just not quite on the terms or in the ways I envisioned.

It was the beginning of 2008 and I had signed up to go on a missions trip to Haiti with a team of people. At this point, my business was growing but one of our partners had stolen a large amount of money from the business several months back, which caused financial stress on the business as well as on my personal finances. I was extremely overextended and was barely making ends meet. Our job as a mission's team member was to raise the money we needed to go on the mission trip, otherwise you could be cut from the team. I remember the day the pastor called me into the office and told me, "you are short on your fundraising so if enough money does not come in collectively you may not be able to go."

I was devastated. My plan was to fund entire mission trips and here I was, looking at being cut from the team for not having enough funds to cover myself. Thankfully, God raised the money from somewhere and I was able to go with the team to Haiti.

While in Haiti, our job was to help build a new church building in the Cape Haitian area. Needless to say, you cannot go to an area like Haiti and not be impacted by the poverty and hopelessness those people were living in. Because of the language barrier, I spent most of my time playing with the kids and did some random construction for the building whenever the need arose. Overall, it was a great trip and I was happy I made the cut to go. I saw God working through our team and the impact we were having on that community. As our ten day trip came to an end, the Haitian pastor gave out cards to all the team members thanking us for our service to the Lord. I had not spoken to him very much because of the language barrier so I appreciated the card. As I opened the card I read these words, "You remind my wife and I of Job." I was baffled by this because Job had some struggles to say the least, but

I did not give it much thought at the time. I certainly had no idea why this pastor had written those words to me.

When I got home I went back to work. My partner and I were looking at the numbers and our business was simply not making ends meet. I was behind on all my bills, personal and business. Most of the debt was in my name because my partner had bad credit (first warning sign) and could not get the credit needed to invest in the business. In the weeks after returning from Haiti, my house phone rang off the hook from multiple creditors. It got so bad that my wife and I decided to disconnect our phone. I was clinging to this business for dear life because I was convinced that it was my way forward to get to seminary: make a lot of money and use it to serve God. After all, God had a plan for me right?

It was a Saturday night and the next day after Sunday service all the team members who went to Haiti were going to give a five minute testimony of how the trip impacted them to the congregation. As I sat downstairs that night in my living room, the reality set in hard and fast that my financial situation was falling apart. Fear set in because I had a wife and three kids depending on me to provide for them and that seemed to be impossible. I hit my knees and tears started rolling down my face and I prayed, "God you can have it all! Just show me what you want me to do! I will do whatever you want! Just take care of my family."

Have you ever heard the term "be careful what you pray for"? Well, I would end up being a perfect example of that. God would not only answer that prayer, He would do it very quickly.

The next day I did my five minute presentation and after everyone else was done, my family and I made our way upstairs. The pastor came running up to me out of breath and said, "I have been looking all over for you! God put it on my heart to tell you that you are ordained to preach His word!" I was a bit taken aback but quickly realized God answered my prayer from the previous night very quickly. God knew I needed to hear that, but He also knew He needed to prepare me to do it. He would ultimately take me up on the "You can have it all" portion of my prayer. It was the how he would prepare me for His work that I had yet to see. My plan of being the top donor at our church ended abruptly when I had to ask the deacons at our church to help me make my mortgage payment. I was so far behind that I was going to lose my house any day. It is important to say that throughout this time I continued to serve God, which was the anchor I needed to help me keep seeking Him. I was the Junior High Sunday school teacher and I started a ministry for people with addictions at our church. I was also sharing my testimony with people who were going through the same struggles I was having at the time. I do not say this to puff myself up. I say it because God was using me whether I liked it or not, or whether I knew it or not.

It was August 2008 when those words "You remind me of Job" started to make sense and come to reality in many ways. I found out early in the month that our business lost another large account; this was the third or fourth one in a row. Not only did we lose it, they were not even going to pay us for the work we did. This would be the final blow that would spiral our business finances to a breaking point. The reality finally set in that the business simply could not sustain itself and the inevitable was fast approaching. The business would have to be shut down and my master plan would be crushed.

We unhooked our house phone due to the relentless calls from creditors. Our mailbox was overflowing with daily reminders of the inevitable. We became too petrified to even answer our cell phones and could not summons the courage to open up the mail. I was depressed, sad, hopeless, and felt like a complete failure as a Father, husband, and Christian. My entire world was being stripped from me and I did not know where to turn. I knew what was happening, but I could not grasp why. I became angry with God because He was allowing this to happen and was messing up my plan.

In the middle of August my mom became very ill two days after my dad came home from the hospital and was recovering from surgery. A week after finding out my mom was ill, my partner and I decided to close down shop for good. There was no money left. We could not even put gas in our trucks to get to the jobs, never mind purchasing the materials to complete them.

A few days after my mom became ill, she ended up in the hospital. It was not looking good for her and I think we all sensed that she may not come home. My dad gave me the awful task of asking my mom where she wanted to be buried just in case she did not make it home. Her wishes unfortunately would be granted a few days later when she passed away.

So as my personal and company trucks were getting repossessed and foreclosure notices were coming in, we were also trying to help my father with arrangements for my mom's funeral. I had no job, my mom died, trucks were being repossessed, we were broke, and I was trying to grieve my mother's death, all within about a two-week time period. It was a trying time to say the least.

I would be remiss not to share God's mercy, love and grace during this time. My wife and mother did not get along for years before her death. The last few weeks before she passed away, my wife started taking care of my mom. She would change, clean, and dress her almost every day. It got to a point where the only person my mom wanted to help her was my wife and would call for her when she was not there. God restored the relationship between my wife and my mom beyond where it was before the differences arose. My father and I were never close, but during this time our relationship began to deepen, and God's healing was starting to take hold. God was repairing broken relationships even in the midst of the current storms in my life.

It was the end of August and my wife informed me that we had $60 left in our bank account. My heart sank because I had no idea what I was going to do. My job search was not amounting to much, and quite frankly, I was just tired and discouraged over the events of the past few months. We came up with the idea to have a garage sale to try and make enough money to at least buy food for a couple of weeks. During our garage sale one of my friends called and asked if he could bring us lunch. I said "sure," and about two hours later he showed up with a minivan filled with groceries. I cannot tell you the relief and joy I had, knowing my family would have food for the next few weeks at least. I think it's fair to say at the average garage sale people make $300 to $400 if they are lucky. Not only had God supplied food for the next few weeks through my friend, we ended up making over $2,000 that day at our garage sale. God was beginning to teach me that He would provide for our needs, we just had to trust Him.

It was about that same time I would make the decision that actually led to the book you are currently reading. I was sitting upstairs on my computer looking for work when I came across an Army website. I always wanted to be a Paratrooper so I checked out the website. This was during the 2008 surge for the war in Afghanistan and the Army was taking people up to the age of 40 years old and I was 37. I thought about it for a minute and decided

I would give it a try and see what happened. I told my wife my plan and she did not seem all that excited, but being the loving supportive wife, she said, "go check it out I guess."

The next day I was down in the recruiter's office. I took the pre-entry test to see what jobs I qualified for. I told the recruiter I wanted Airborne Infantry. If I was going to war I wanted to be on the front lines not stuck in the rear. Most people around me thought I was crazy but I looked at it and thought, my family will have housing, medical, and an income, and if I die they will get $450,000--it seemed logical to me. I was 37 years old when I signed up for the Army to become a Paratrooper but what I was in store for only God knew.

I think it's important to say I was angry with God during this period of time. Yes, I was still serving Him at our church--but How could He let this happen to me! Here I was, trying to set MYSELF up to do His work and I thought He smacked me in the face. When I signed the line for the Army I grumbled to myself, "Well God, I guess you'll have to wait 20 years until my military career is over until I preach." I know it sounds ridiculous but that's how I was feeling. I loved God, but it really angered me that He allowed all this to happen. I am, as we all are, living proof that His ways are truly greater than ours. What God did to me, for me, and through me in the upcoming chapters is truly a Testament to the fact that He is the Perfect Father.

Job 13:15 reads, "Though He slay me, yet I will trust Him. Even so, I will defend my own ways before Him." At this point, Job had lost all his possessions, his children were dead, he was covered in boils and his wife suggested he curse God and die. In addition, his friends were accusing him, claiming that all that was happening to him was his fault. Therefore, what he proclaims in verse 15 is so remarkable, "Though He slay me, yet I will trust in Him." In other words, Job was saying that even if God were to kill him, he would still trust Him. The Greek word used here for the phrase "Yet I will trust" is *Yachal,* which carries with it not just the idea of trust, but of hope and expectation. Think of it... Job had lost it all and amid his suffering he was still hoping, waiting and trusting in God!

God uses the circumstances in our lives to refine us and conform us into the image of His son. Much like gold is refined of its impurities through fire, tough times in the crucible of God's fire refines us for the task ahead. At this time, we may find ourselves begging God to turn down the flame, thinking the fire is too hot for us to endure. But God, the Master Potter is firing the kiln to just the right temperature to accomplish His plan in our lives. Not so high that He destroys us and not so low that it contains no lasting effect. In the end turning out a vessel meet and sincere for the Master's use.

Precious Lord, though I may not understand all the circumstances I am facing, I am confident that you are working things out to accomplish your purpose in my life. Help me to respond like job, with hope and expectation, trusting in you. My greatest desire is to be used of you, refine me, purify me and make me into a vessel sincere and ready to bring you Glory.

AAR (after action report) Reflection:

1. Have you ever felt like Job, pressed on all sides? How did you respond?

2. How does the understanding of God's refining fire give you courage to face the future?

Chapter 2

"God either is, or He is not"

We have all seen movies about Military Basic Training, more commonly known as "Boot Camp." While most depictions are somewhat accurate, the actual experience is something that cannot by conveyed on a movie screen, and it leaves a lasting impact. The lessons I learned during these training environments were extremely valuable and life-changing. My ability to persevere and remain focused on the task at hand was certainly enhanced through these events. What I would experience through my training would change how I viewed God's call in my life and prepare me for the mission He was laying before me.

I guess you could say I was hardheaded, because I had the "pleasure" of experiencing "Boot Camp" three times in my life, four if you were to include the police academy. Allow me to explain: when I was 17 years old, I joined the Army National Guard. I wanted to join the regular Army, but back in 1989, recruiters were like used car salesmen. I unknowingly walked into the National Guard Recruiting Office by mistake and a pile of broken promises later, I ended up in the National Guard for my first "Boot Camp."

I can assure you I had not planned on returning to "Boot Camp" almost 20 years later. As I stated in the previous chapter, I joined the Army in November of 2008 after the loss of my business. My first training stop was a six week "Boot Camp" for prior service soldiers. That was "Boot Camp" number two.

Afterwards, I headed to Infantry school in Fort Benning, Georgia for what was supposed to be four weeks of infantry training. At the time, Infantry School and Boot Camp were combined for new soldiers, who attended nine weeks of regular Boot Camp, immediately followed by infantry school, for a total of twelve weeks.

When I arrived at Fort Benning, I was supposed to be inserted for the last four weeks of the twelve-week cycle. As fate would have it, I was inserted into the 4th week of the cycle, which meant I had eight more weeks of "Boot Camp." That brings me to my third round of Boot Camp. Police Academy would come six years later at age 43 after serving my time in the Military.

I guess I was a "Glutton for Punishment" and thick headed--I will leave that for you the reader to decide. While it was certainly challenging, especially at my age, those training experiences were a vital part of teaching me teamwork and perseverance. Looking back, I would do it all over again in a heartbeat.

I left my family for basic training on November 8, 2008. It was a cold November morning; the recruiter picked me up at 3:30 am and took me to Fort Dix, New Jersey to be shipped out for my first round of training. I will never forget looking out that car window and waving goodbye to my family as I drove off into the unknown. I was tired and emotionally drained from all the events of the last few months.

I was angry at God, mad at myself, and I could not understand how I ended up at this point in my life. There was a peace through knowing that at least I had a paycheck and a guaranteed job for the next three plus years. Beyond that, I had no idea what God had in store for me or my family over the next few years. What I didn't know is I was exactly where God wanted me. I was coming to the end of myself and my way of thinking. I was broken, beat up, tired, and helpless. This was exactly where God needed me to be, so He could continue refining and preparing me for His work.

What's funny about trying to prepare mentally for the upcoming training is all new soldiers and even old ones say the same things to ourselves before getting in front of the dreaded Drill Sergeant. "I am not going to let anything they say get to me. It's all just a show. They are just trying break you!" I can tell you from my experience, no matter how many times you say that to yourself it does not work! They find ways to get to you and no matter how hard you try or how many times you have been through it, when a Drill SGT. gets in your face, you know it. Here I was, 37 years old with a past resume as a manager, regional manager, divisional manager, business owner and father of three children, getting told by a 23 year old Drill Sgt. "I was worthless, I was a failure, I had no clue about life, and that I would never make it in his Army!" I know this may sound horrible, but I was full of pride and anger, and quite honestly, it was what I needed at the time. God was using the verbal and physical beatings to assist me in the realization that I had no idea what was good for me and lacked the humility to be used by Him.

The harder they pushed me physically and mentally, the harder I tried and the more determined I became to push through. I was determined to not let them break me. I remember one Drill Sgt. Saying "Hey Grandpa! I am going to break you off!"

I can say now that I regret the next two words that came out of my mouth. "Bring it!" I said. I instantly thought to myself "Oops!"

The Drill SGT. Took me up on my challenge and I spent the next three hours carrying two filled five-gallon water jugs up and down three flights of stairs. When that was completed, I was doing pushups and sit-ups with two full duffle bags of clothing inside. I had so much anger, rage, and pride in my heart that this was like rocket fuel for me. I guess God, through my Drill Sgt., was allowing me to burn off my rage. I ended up in front of a doctor two days later because I could not feel my fingers after carrying those jugs for three hours. I guess pride does come before the fall.

I think in the beginning of my training I operated and endured on pure anger, rage, and pride. As I stated, I was angry at God and myself. But in the midst of this, something beautiful was happening as my training dragged on week after week. My anger, rage, and pride began to burn off and break off. God was replacing it with something much more valuable and useful to Him: weakness and humility. After the rage, anger, and pride subsided I was forced to draw the strength and perseverance I needed not from myself but from God. And God's strength was not fueled by anger, rage, and pride but by love, grace, and mercy. As I leaned on Him more and more, my physical and emotional pain became secondary and was no longer an obstacle that impeded me. I learned it was not the Drill Sgt. breaking me down, it was God creating a need for Himself in me. It was through my brokenness that I was being made new and started gaining the ability to listen and learn. This would be just the beginning of a lifelong refining and renewing process.

It was during this time that I began to see I was bankrupt without God and there was a peace in knowing that. The load of self-manufacturing a Master plan for my life and how I would serve God was lifted. God's plan was not some sort of riddle that I had to try and figure out, His plan was His plan and my job was to submit to it.

The more I got into God's Word (the Bible) during my time in training, the more I started to see that God was using the Army to draw me closer to Him and focus on the mission instead of myself. It was all starting to make sense as time went on. The constant yelling, lack of food, sleep deprivation, and physical exhaustion all had a purpose in taking a broken man and making a soldier out of him, not only in the US Army but in God's Army. Everything in the military is about one thing: the mission. You are given a task as a platoon or squad and each person had a job to do. If someone failed at their job, the mission could be compromised and the objective might not be achieved, which meant people could die. If a soldier was too tired to carry his gear, we would split it up among other soldiers and continue on with the mission. If a soldier quit, he was left behind because the mission came first and you were either a part of completing it or you were an obstacle to achieving it. Each member of a squad, platoon, or unit had a purpose and your physical comfort and even personal safety were not the primary concern--the mission was. I learned that these principles also apply to the mission we are given by God. I began to learn that I was placing my needs and comforts before the God's plan for my life. I was not seeking His plan but my selfish agenda.

As time went on, the bonds between us soldiers began to grow. We all had a common purpose and if one failed, we all failed. We needed each other to complete the work set before us. The yelling, exhaustion, and hunger became mere background noise as we began to focus on the mission more than ourselves. It was a beautiful picture of how God intended His believers to work together.

Christ said, "Pick up your Cross and Follow me!"

Our Drill Sgt. yelled, "pick up your gear and follow me!"

I was starting to see that God's purpose and mission were greater than the worldly trials that were going on in my life. If I fixed my eyes on God, His purpose, and mission, everything else would become background noise and would not distract me. As soldiers in training we were preparing for "GOING TO WAR." Every soldier in that Boot Camp would be in combat within the next 12 months. Our lives would depend on our ability to trust one another and submit ourselves to our leader's orders and guidance to accomplish the mission. We were not a one man Army, we were a team and a brotherhood. Our orders came from above and our leaders were entrusted with the task and duty of making sure those orders were carried out. Our job was to do our part and submit to our leaders so we could complete the mission return home safely.

I remember many late evenings cleaning our weapons and packing our "rucksacks" (large backpacks) and then double and triple checking to make sure we had the supplies needed for the next day. Since the Army was only required to give you four hours of sleep, that meant that most nights you sacrificed sleep to prepare for the next day's mission. I was learning how to sacrifice for the greater good. I was learning to look beyond myself and keep my eyes fixed on what was to be accomplished instead of my personal preference or comfort. These lessons, when filtered through the lens of God's refining, would become valuable assets as I began to submit more to His plan rather than my own.

I remember doing a Land Navigation training mission towards the end of Infantry School. The mission was simple but not easy. It started with a seven mile Ruck March into the woods with just over one-hundred pounds of gear overall. Most of the weight was in your Ruck, which you carried on your back, but between your weapon, bullets, armor plated vest and helmet, it added up to an easy 100 pounds. They set us up into ten man squads and gave each squad a map and a compass. When we arrived at the middle of nowhere in the woods we were told to set up our fighting positions. Setting up a fighting position was simple: dig a hole big enough to lay down in. Fighting positions were dual purpose because they were also your living quarters. No tents were issued but you were allowed to use your issued poncho to keep your weapon and gear dry. We would sleep at this location one night and then the next morning set out with our maps and compasses to find the objective they had marked for us on the map.

Our squad got up early that morning and set out on our mission. As we left, we quickly realized that most other squads went in a different direction. That should have been a good indicator that we were off to a bad start. It only was supposed to take three hours to reach the objective according to the timetable given to us. After about seven hours of Ruck Marching through the woods with all our gear, the realization set in that we made a wrong turn. We were all getting very tired and were starting to run out of ideas of how to find the objective. We were on our own, there was no Drill Sgt. to help just us find our way. After almost eight hours we finally came across a road and felt relieved to be out of the woods, literally. We decided our best and easiest option would be to follow the road and hopefully come across someone or something that would help us. After about an hour on the road a truck came by with a Drill Sgt. He welcomed us by using some choice words regarding our intelligence and map reading abilities. That was the first time any of us were happy to see and hear the words of our Drill Sgt.

He hopped out of the truck and said, "You are all a bunch of Idiots! You couldn't find your way out of a paper bag." After checking our water supply and making sure there were no injuries he said, "follow me!"

We followed him for almost another five hours. I was marching in the front of our squad and holding my own until hour five came. I was praying because I had never fallen out on a Ruck March or any other physical challenge, but at this point I was simply running out of steam. I had nothing left. My legs started to slow down and my heart began to sink because I knew it was just a matter of time until I would stop. I could not catch my breath as I struggled to keep going. I moved over to the side of the road to allow others to pass me and I became convinced that I was not going to make it. No sooner did I think that when the Drill SGT shouted, "You are at the objective, set up camp in that wood line!"

The relief and joy I felt were unbelievable. God knew exactly how much gas I had in the tank and when it would run out. You cannot train perseverance, it is a byproduct of putting your comfort and pain aside, because you understand the purpose is bigger than you. You draw your strength to keep moving forward, not from yourself, but from God and those around you. I did not fall out of the march because I was strong but because God knew just how far He could take me before I needed to rest. We reached our objective and accomplished the mission given to us. This experience was awesome because I could see how God was using that training mission to show me He will give us the strength we need to accomplish the work He has set before us.

Had I listened to my physical pain, I would have stopped. Had I listened to my mind, I would have stopped. Instead, I kept my eyes on the mission set before me and trusted that if I kept moving and was willing to endure just a little more I would arrive, and I did. **Praise God!**

Infantry School was coming to an end, and as tired and beat up as I was physically and mentally, I was no longer consumed with the rage, anger, and pride I had when I started. Our last task before officially completing Infantry School was a 16 mile Ruck March with all our gear. Once this march was completed you earned the blue Infantry Cord which signified you were an Infantryman.

It was 16 degrees when we started our march and even though it was cold, we were dripping with sweat. It was so cold that sweat froze on my face and I had icicles hanging from my nose and eyebrows during most of the march. Nothing can truly prepare you for walking 16 miles with 100 pounds of gear. Your body simply is not designed to do that. But anyone who has done this type of thing will understand what I am about to say. You hit a point during this type of event where your body and mind separate. Your legs just keep going with no thought, almost as if they are on autopilot. You mentally began to go into an almost hypnotic state during these long marches.

Have you ever been driving and not remembered how you got there? That's what happens to your mind during these long marches. We were less than a mile from the finish line when I marched into a pothole. My ankle rolled and because my Ruck Sack was so heavy I fell face first onto the gravel road. I was down, and I was down good. I started seeing blood dripping from my face onto the road and was trying to figure out where it was coming from.

A soldier came to help me but the Drill Sgt. yelled at him "Keep going! The mission does not end because we have a soldier down!"

This sounds heartless, but I understood. I knew through my training that the mission came first. The Drill Sgt. asked me as I laid there bleeding from my face, "Lee, you have less than a mile to go! You have to finish with your platoon to earn your Blue Infantry Cord! Can you do it?"

I asked God for the strength to push through and He answered me immediately. I got up and started running. I ran about a quarter mile until I caught up to my platoon and took my place in rank. God had given me the strength and endurance to complete that march and I earned my Blue Infantry Cord. I knew in my heart the Cord was God's not mine, but I was thankful He allowed me to wear it for Him.

My next stop right after infantry school was Airborne School which was only a three week school. After completion, I would be an Airborne Infantryman and earn my Jump Wings. I would also earn the right to wear a Red Beret signifying I was a Paratrooper. The school itself was not physically hard. My faith in what God could do through me was growing and I felt confident with the fact that He had my back.

It is important to say I was scared of heights. I know, "Why would you sign up to jump out of planes if you are afraid of heights?" I wish I had a good answer, but I think it's because I did not want my fear to determine what I did and I wanted the title Paratrooper.

After two weeks of training it was jump time. Sixty paratroopers entered a C-130. The plane would make two passes over the drop zone. When we arrived, 15 paratroopers had 30 seconds to jump out of each side of the airplane. Our group was in line to jump on the second pass. As we made the first pass my heart was pounding out of my chest. I watched as the first group stood up, hooked up, and headed to the door. The red light changed to green and I watched those soldiers jump out of the airplane within 30 seconds. As I sat there amazed that those guys jumped out of the plane, I heard our group saying, "I can't believe they actually just jumped out!" Within a few seconds the reality set in that we were next.

As I stood and hooked up my static line (that is what deploys your parachute), my legs began to tremble and I was afraid I would freeze at the door and not jump. Then I thought about what God had done so far in my life. I remembered all He had taught me throughout my training. As the plane came over the drop zone and the red light turned green, I thought to myself as I made my way to the door, "God either is or God is not. If God is, then whether the chute opens or not, I am good. If God is not, then no matter what happens I am screwed."

I came to the door and jumped, trusting that the results were God's not mine and that I would be OK regardless of what happened. My first jump was my best jump, I landed like a feather. My other jumps during my tour would not be so cozy, but God is, was, and will always be. We only need to trust Him and follow Him through the fear, pain, exhaustion, and hunger, and He will give us the strength to accomplish the work He has set out for us to do.

"God either is or He is not." Once we settle that question, the rest is for His glory. We read in 2 Timothy 2:3-4, "You therefore must endure hardship as a good soldier of Jesus Christ. No one engaged in warfare entangles himself with the affairs of this life, that he may please him who enlisted him as a soldier."

Paul was reminding Timothy that he was an enlisted soldier in the army of Christ. The mission ahead would not be easy, it would be difficult and dangerous. He would have to endure many hardships, as evidenced by Paul's own example, but such is the cost of serving the King. This letter to Timothy is traditionally considered the last of Paul's writings. He had paid the price, he recognized that his time was nearing.

"For I am already being poured out as a drink offering, and the time of my departure is at hand. I have fought the good fight, I have finished the race, I have kept the faith. Finally, there is laid up for me the crown of righteousness, which the Lord, the righteous Judge will give to me on that day, and not to me only but also to all who have loved His appearing." (2 Timothy 4:6-8)

You see, he was charging Timothy to finish the mission. It is true that God's mercy, grace, and unconditional love saves us from the eternal consequences of our sin, but in exchange He enlists us as soldiers in His army and then charges us with a mission, a mission we must complete at all costs.

"Go, therefore and make disciples of all nations, baptizing them in the name of the Father and of the Son and of the Holy Spirit, teaching them to observe all things that I have commanded you; and lo, I am with you always, even to the end of the age." (Matthew 28:19-20)

"God either is or He is not," have you settled this question? If so, the call is clear, and the mission laid bare. Are you ready?....

Father, forgive me if I have allowed the cares of this world to entangle me and keep me from your primary call. Help me to endure as a good soldier in your service. Strengthen me when I am weak. When I am discouraged and tired remind me of my mission. As I wait upon you, ready me for the battle. Fill me with your power, with your presence and with your passion for the lost. Amen.

AAR Reflections:

1. God either is or is not, have you settled the question? What is it that you need to leave in His hands?

2. Why do you think it is so difficult to "jump" out of the plane and into God's will?

Chapter 3

"What was that noise Daddy?"

It was December 7, 2009; my little girls 8th birthday. I was stationed in Vicenza, Italy with the 173rd Airborne Infantry Brigade. My unit was making final preparations for our 1 year deployment to Afghanistan. We were scheduled to ship out on December 9th: two days after my daughters 8th birthday. My daughter celebrated her birthday that year in Venice, which was only about a 30 minute drive from our base. I felt so blessed to be there for her birthday. As you can imagine, she was thrilled to be celebrating her birthday at St. Mark's Square in Venice. She was even more thrilled to be staying at a 5 star hotel in the square with my wife, stepson, and sister-in-law. It is hard to describe the feeling you have when you are celebrating your little girl's birthday with family, knowing that this may be the last time you get to do that. I could not spend the night in Venice with my family because we were not allowed to stay off base during the weeks prior to our deployment. I left early that night and took a water taxi through Venice back to the parking area. I remember riding through Venice on the boat and wondering, "is this the last birthday that I will be with my daughter? Where will I be a year from now? Will my family be heading back to the States without me?" I am confident most soldiers feel this way before going to war and I don't wish those feelings on anyone.

The battle would start in my heart and mind before I even left. I thought back to the months of training and tried to recall the things I was taught and what I was trained for. My mind went blank as I tried to remember all I had been taught. The inevitable fact remained that not everyone who went was coming back. It wasn't a morbid thought, just the reality of war. I knew God had me in the palm of His hand. I also knew He would take care of my family, but I would be lying if I did not say I was scared by the thought that this might be my last moment of joy with my family until Heaven.

The day came when it was time to leave for Afghanistan. Our Company met in the assembly area for formation. We had our lives packed in two duffle bags, a Ruck Sack (large backpack) and an Assault bag (small backpack). Now the time had come to say our final good-byes to our families. I stood before my wife, stepson, and daughter and struggled to find the proper words to say goodbye. It's not like I was leaving to go camping for the weekend. I was leaving for a year for the front lines in Afghanistan to a place called the Tangi Valley. I gave my hugs and kisses and then our Commander said those words, "form it up!" (short for getting the platoon into formation). The hardest thing to do was turning and walking away from them while fighting back tears. I was desperately trying to burn the memory of their faces into my head, hoping those images would last until I saw them again.

John Lee

I told my daughter these words before I left. "Pumpkin, don't
worry you can't kill a Christian. I am either coming home to be
with you or going home to be with the Lord." I can honestly tell
you I believed those words. I took comfort in that truth, rested in
that truth, and drew my strength in that truth. The experience of
leaving was difficult, but it was a necessary step of faith that God
would use to accomplish the work he needed to do in me and
through me. He would also use this time apart to strengthen my
family for the plans and mission He had for them.

As we made our way to Afghanistan I was able to email and
call my family on a somewhat regular basis. The closer we got to
our final stop in the Tangi valley the harder it became to reach out
to them. It took about a week from the time I left Italy to make it to
our new home for the next year, Combat Outpost Tangi or what we
referred to as C.O.P. Tangi. I was now officially thousands of
miles away from my family on the front lines in Afghanistan.

I can tell you with certainty there is nothing more important
than speaking, writing, or getting packages from your family when
you are deployed. Mail day was a big day for us, especially
because it was so hard to get supplies out to our valley. The safest
way in or out was by helicopter and even that had its issues. Every
time we knew the mail was being flown in we all waited anxiously,
hoping to get something. The feeling could be best summed up by
comparing it to an 8 year old kid on Christmas morning waiting to
open his gifts. There was nothing more precious for me than

opening hand drawn pictures, handwritten notes, or anything else that had the scent and feel of home on it. At one point I asked my Father-in-Law to mail a sandwich bag with some American soil from his backyard. I remember the day when it finally arrived and I could not wait to open the bag and smell that dirt. It may sound strange, but there was nothing more beautiful to me than the smell of that American soil. I carried that sandwich bag in my left front breast pocket throughout my deployment. Next to God and family, there was nothing more precious to me than that soil.

As remote and limited as our base was, we did have a few computers with internet and some phones that we used to call home and email our families. The high point of my week was speaking to my loved ones, either in the States or in Italy where our base was. There was nothing more beautiful than hearing those sweet soft voices of the ones you loved. It was like a burst of fresh air compared to the sounds of war we constantly experienced. There were times I would speak to my family and listen to their struggles but not be able to do anything to help or comfort them. Those conversations were the hardest to deal with because ultimately there was nothing you could do except comfort them with words from thousands of miles away. This is where the deep bonds started to develop and set in among the soldiers I served with. We all shared the same struggles. We all missed someone, and we were all going to do our best to help each other get home to see that someone. We often shared our struggles or the struggles our families were having back at home with one another. I remember the call from my wife when she told me that our car broke down on the way home about an hour away from the Aviano Air Base. It was a $500 beater car, so the cost of the tow would have cost twice as much as the car was worth. As she shared this with me, I began to feel panic and frustration, knowing there was nothing I could do but listen. It quickly became clear that God was working in her life and He was taking care of my family. She tried to reassure me and said, "It's fine I can use the base shuttle, get a ride, or walk." What amazed me was that I could hear the complete peace she had with it. I could see how her faith had grown. She knew that God had a plan and that they would be just fine. If I stopped the story there that would be encouraging enough, but God had His own finish that neither one of us could have known or even imagined. I spoke to my wife again about a week later and I could hear the excitement in her voice. She said to me, "You are not going to believe what just happened! One of the ladies from church called me and said she needed some help picking up groceries at the base commissary (food store). She asked me if I could I meet her there. When I showed up at the commissary there was an older man standing there with my friend. He told me that he heard what happened to our car. He also explained that his wife had terminal cancer and when she heard a soldier's wife was in need she immediately wanted to help. He then said how he and his wife decided they did not need her car anymore since she could not drive and wanted us to have it. The man then handed me the keys and title to a PT Cruiser with 30,000 miles on it and walked away." I was blown away and as consumed with joy as she was. God knew what was needed and provided it. God also knew I needed the comfort of knowing my family had transportation. He also wanted to bless my wife for her faithfulness and fulfill the need she had for a car. God saw fit through His love to provide us what we needed through a man that was losing his wife to cancer. You just can't make this stuff up. If you ask me, I think God was showing off a bit.

There are no holidays or weekends when you are in a war zone. Since we deployed in early December, I spent Christmas of 2009 away from my family. My wife waited to tell me until after I came home how empty that Christmas felt as they opened gifts with no dad around. I spent my Christmas that year watching a Taliban prisoner we detained for his involvement in an IED attack just a few days before. It was a long cold Christmas for me that year. I tried to imagine that I was home with my family as they opened their gifts. I tried to remember the images of those beautiful faces I saw the day I left to come to this dark place.

It was in that sadness and longing for family and friends that something remarkable began to take place for me. Being separated from my family forced me to understand that they were God's, not mine. God in His love and mercy entrusted them to me while on this Earth. While I was apart from them, I realized I was left with God, my Bible, my Battle Buddies, and the mission. My time away was forcing me and my family to trust God for our strength and provision instead of ourselves. It was remarkable how God was refining us through this time we were separated.

I think one of the hardest parts about the conversations with family was not letting them in on what was going on. Being in an active war zone changes you and your perspective on things. In most cases, when you are speaking to a loved one they may ask, "How was your day?" It is a simple and common question in most cases unless you are in an active war zone. You never want to tell them how your day really was for many reasons. First, you don't want them to worry any more than they already are. Can you imagine answering that innocent question with, "Great, we took two RPG rounds but thankfully no one was injured. I only sleep four hours a night and the food is horrible. Oh, and I sure hope we get a water supply soon because I have been wearing the same T-shirt for three weeks and would like to rinse it with some clean water." This would not be the best response to a "How was your day" question. However, there is another response that is not good either, as I soon would learn. When you are deployed you see and experience life and death situations on most days, and to cope at some point you begin to become hardened to your new normal. I remember my wife asking me, "So what did you do today?" My response at the time I thought was innocent enough. " Well," I said, "This Afghan soldier went out to buy some bread from the village and he got shot in the head with a .22 caliber round! When he walked on base to see the doc (that's what we called medics) The doc said to him, 'Dude you just got shot in the head!' The guy was fine. The bullet did not penetrate his skull so doc just pulled it out." I chuckling as I told her this because for us this was a funny story with a happy ending. My wife however, was not as amused as I assumed she would be and said, "That's not funny, he could have died. Please don't turn into something you are not." I learned quickly that the world I was living in was different from hers and anyone else's that I knew back home. Our conversations going forward remained focused on their world not mine, and I did my best to filter what I said to them about what was happening. War has a way of breaking through that filter at times no matter how hard you try to keep it out. I remember speaking with my daughter one night. She had the sweetest little voice. While we were talking, suddenly a loud explosion shook the phone tent and then I heard her say, "What was that noise Daddy?" As my heart was pounding I said, " Nothing pumpkin, but Daddy has to go now." Thankfully, it was the sound of our mortars firing at the enemy and not the enemy firing at us. The sound of war found its way through and my daughter was on the receiving end.

As the middle of my deployment grew near, our conversations began to center around what we were going to do when I got my two week leave. In the Army if you deploy more than six months, you get a two week leave, or as we call it, R&R. During this time the Army would fly you wherever you wanted to go, free of charge.

My wife and I decided to spend that time together back in New Jersey where we had left just a year before. I was so excited that that the time was drawing near when I could see them again. I had spoken to my son who lived in North Carolina from my first marriage, and he would be meeting us in New Jersey. The church we left was gracious enough to allow us to stay at their parsonage during my leave. Our plans seemed to be coming together nicely and I could not wait to see them. While my conversations with my family were filled with excitement, there was lurking in the background another test of faith. I felt uncomfortable saying to them, "I will see you in a couple weeks!" because honestly, who really knew if I would except God. At this point, we were starting to see a lot more combat and things were heating up more and more with each passing day. My prayers became, "God just let me see them one more time. If you want to take me that's fine, but wait until after I see them this one last time." So the excitement was impeded by my fear that God may take me home before I got to see them.

During my deployment I found out that my father had cancer again and it was quickly getting worse. Of course, whenever I talked to him he would always try to reassure me that everything would be fine and that he looked forward to seeing me when I came back. I think we both knew that his time was growing short as each day passed. I was burdened and saddened by the reality that my father was dying and there was a chance that either he would go before I could see him or I could go before he could see me. I want to be clear at this point, nobody has a guarantee on tomorrow, that's in God's hands not ours. Certainly my faith was being tested during this time and I had to leave the uncertainties up to God.

I remember the last time I talked to my father. It was about two weeks before I was supposed to come home on leave. We had the greatest conversation I could ever remember having with him. He was so happy to hear from me and felt so blessed that my son was coming back in the states to visit with him. He sounded great! I could feel his joy pouring through the phone. After hanging up the phone I began walking back to the chow tent. It was then that my heart sank, and I just knew God had blessed the two of us with our best and last conversation. Then I said to myself, "It's OK dad, you can let go now." I just knew God was calling him home. Two days later I got the news that he was in bad shape and they did not know how much longer he was going to make it. I let my commander know and called my wife. He was able to push up my plans from two weeks to right away. The Battalion Commander diverted his two blackhawk helicopters to our outpost so I could begin my journey home. To see the love and support from my unit was inspiring and God knew I needed that comfort at that time. I have to say it was an awesome experience to be flying what is called "map of the earth" (which means low and fast) as I looked and saw the door gunner hanging out the side of the Blackhawk, while in the distance I could see another Blackhawk flying offset to us. It was like being in a movie I once saw. I arrived at Bagram Air Force Base that following morning at about 3 a.m. I immediately found a computer to let everyone know where I was and when I would be leaving Afghanistan. It was then I saw the email from my ex-wife saying, "I am so sorry, John, your father passed away just a few hours ago."

I just stared at the screen and fought back the tears. At that point I had not slept in almost 24 hours, and as I sat at that computer time seemed to stand still. I got up after a few minutes and just walked to my temporary bunk and laid there. I thought to myself, *Here I am two days away from seeing my family and so excited, yet filled with sorrow that I missed seeing my father before he passed*. Talk about a confusing period of time. Full of joy, sorrow, excitement, mourning, happy, mad, glad, relieved to be off the front lines and ready to cry. That was an interesting combination to experience all at once and one I would not wish on my worst enemy. How do I grieve when I am seeing the people I love for the first time in six months, knowing that I only have two weeks to be with them before I have to leave again for another six months? How could I possibly spend my time enjoying my family while making preparations for my father's funeral?

These are not questions I can answer, but God can and did. I thought about my conversation just days before when I spoke with my father. He was so consumed with joy in His heart that it traveled halfway around the world and brought me joy, comfort, and peace. I knew it was God that had given me and my father a beautiful last moment together on this side of eternity. The time on leave with my family was amazing and wonderful despite the grief and busyness. God's restoration power is beyond our comprehension and emotions. My relationship with my father was never more intimate than when we were a half-a-world apart. God's restoration power is not limited by distance, space, or time.

When facing life's uncertainties, our trust in God and His goodness provides us with a way forward. God is sovereign and He knows what we need and when we need it. In the heat of the battle, it is easy for us to lose sight of this. In Luke 12:7 we read, "But the very hairs on your head are all numbered. Do not fear therefore; you are of more value than many sparrows." As we learn to lean and trust in God more and more, it becomes easier to rest in His grace. When we face loss and pain, we can rest assured that our Father in Heaven is on watch and is in the process of working out His master plan. You may not find yourself in the Tangi valley anytime soon, facing the uncertainty of never seeing your family again, but listen to the words of Jesus, "...In the world you will have trouble; but be of good cheer, I have overcome the world" (John 16:33).

Dear sovereign God, help me lean on your mercy and grace when times of trouble seem to overwhelm me. Help me to keep my eyes fixed on your goodness and help me to trust in your ways. When I am uncertain and fear what is to come, give me the courage to face what lies ahead, that my life would bring you glory.

AAR Reflection:

1. Think back to a time of uncertainty in your life. How did you manage to overcome it?

2. How does what is written in John 16:33 encourage you to keep up the fight?

Chapter 4

"It's just a mile marker"

I will start this chapter by reflecting back to a time when I was nine years old. How it will be interpreted by some of you may be different, depending on your theological background. I chose to share it with you because it is part of my testimony and because God used it as a way to bring me comfort, and in order to solidify that He knew exactly what He wanted to achieve in and through me during my time in Afghanistan.

At the age of about nine I was laying on my mom's bed just hanging out. I put my hands over my eyes, when suddenly I saw a picture of what appeared to be Jerusalem in biblical times. I describe that image in hindsight because I had no idea what Jerusalem looked like at that time. I remember the image vividly, even to this day. I saw what appeared to be houses made from mud on the side of a valley. It was if I had viewed it while flying over this valley. I was a bit startled and quickly opened my eyes. I never gave too much thought about what I saw, but I never forgot it either. One thing I can say for sure is that image was burned into my memory and would resurface itself again, as you will see in the coming paragraphs.

Our first stop in Afghanistan was Bagram Air Base. This was a very large base and felt more like a small town than a combat zone.

Our stay here would be very brief. This would be the last time we would have basic amenities for six months so we tried to enjoy it while we had it. We left Bagram on a pair of Chinook helicopters two days later. We were heading to Combat Out Post (C.O.P.) Tangi in the Wardack Province. The intelligence we got on the Tangi Valley was that it was a new outpost that was established about four months before we arrived. There was limited power, only two wooden structures and several tents. We were told there was no running water and therefore no showers, laundry, or sewage systems. The outpost laid in the heart of the Tangi Valley, which had a long history of loss of life. It was explained to us that the Russians lost an entire tank division during their time moving through that valley during the 1980s. The outpost was about the size of two football fields and surrounded by Hesco walls (which were basically metal fencing that folded out like an accordion with burlap on the inside and then filled with dirt). Most of the defensive fighting positions were not constructed yet and the base was extremely vulnerable to enemy attacks.

Shortly after taking off from Bagram Air Base we experienced the first sounds of what we were in store for. The rear door gunner of the Chinook started firing his mini-gun off the back of the helicopter at something or someone in the mountain range we were flying through. At that point you could cut the tension in the aircraft with a knife. We had not even landed at our outpost yet and the bullets were flying. After about a half hour flight we arrived at

COP Tangi. The idea was to get you and all your stuff off the helicopter as quickly as possible, before the Helicopter became a target for the insurgents. As I exited the rear of the aircraft I paused for a second and there it was! It was the exact image I saw when I was nine years old. That moment ended quickly because time was of the essence. I would not discover why that image was so important until later in my deployment.

As I scurried off the helicopter with all my gear, catching my breath seemed almost impossible. The outpost was sitting at 6,800 feet above sea level and the air was thin. I lugged my gear to the tent I was assigned. It did not have enough cots and had limited room for a platoon of 40 soldiers and all their gear. I found a corner on the floor to set my gear up and rolled out my sleeping bag. That would be my home for that first night. It was quite an adjustment as I struggled to sleep on the cold hard floor, shoved in the corner. I thought to myself, "This is going to be a long year."

I got the tour of our new base which took only a few minutes. It had a small wood/tent chow hall, five large tents, a wooden TOCC (Tactical Operation Command Center), one porta John, one out house, an ammunition supply bunker, a few Metal shipping containers, and a gym tent. We did however have a MWR (Morale, Welfare, and Recreation) tent which housed a few working phones and a few working computers. It had shower and bathroom trailers that did not have power or a water supply. They were basically decorations or target practice for the enemy. It became evident by looking at some of the equipment it had received damage from incoming rockets and mortars. The unit we were relieving had lost four soldiers during their short time there and several others were injured. The valley was known for its IED's (Improvised Explosive Devices) and these devices were not only designed for vehicles but were also placed on common walking paths and goat trails that targeted our foot patrols. The IED's in the valley, which was about a mile long, were so common that we decided driving was too dangerous, so most of our supplies came in by air. We decided to do our patrols on foot.

As the sun set that first night the temperature dropped to about 16 degrees. There were no heaters and I lived in a tent, which meant the outside temperature matched the inside temperature. The bottom line is it was cold. What I remember most about that first night is the darkness. You could not see your hand in front of your face. Trying to find my way around the base seemed impossible. We had head lamps, but we had to limit their use, otherwise you could become a target. The outhouse was made of wood and it was not the most comfortable or cleanest place to do your business. Since there was no plumbing and no company to call to clean or remove the waste, it was someone's job to take the barrel of waste to the burn pit. This was not a pleasant job and usually given to soldiers who had disciplinary issues. I remember being in shock the first night. I thought about the basics we take for granted that never cross most people's minds. How was I going to shower, shave, and wash my clothes? Our only supply of water were 16 oz bottles flown in by helicopter and we did not want to waste them on bathing or trying to wash clothes because who knew when the next shipment would come in. The first night was definitely the hardest when it came to my hygiene concerns. It's amazing how quickly you adapt to losing the basic things we all too often take for granted. If a soldier ever asks you for baby wipes please send them, because that is how we maintain hygiene in these situations. I developed a schedule for how long I would wear each pair of clothing, including my underwear. Since I had about 20 pairs of socks, I would wear one pair for a day then turn them inside out and hang them up. I would wear the same pair the next day inside out. This gave me forty days of socks and if need be I could go back and wear the one from the beginning again if I was unable to rinse them out. I wore my t-shirts for 7 days which would take me through about 10 weeks before I had to rinse them and go back through the cycle of shirts again. My outer uniform blouse and pants were good for 30 days. These would last me six months before I had to worry about washing them. After 90 days we finally had working showers, but the water came from a nearby river. The supply was limited and a lot of guys got sick from the water because sewage from Kabul was dumped in it miles upstream. Regardless of where that water came from, there was nothing like that first hot shower after 90 days without a bath.

I spent one night in the corner of that first tent. I was then moved with one other soldier to the 12 by 6 foot wide metal storage container. This would be my new home for the next several months. I was moved there because my commander got wind that I knew how to do electric, plumbing, and construction. My mission was to build up the infrastructure of our outpost. My job consisted of 18 to 20 hour days trying to run power, provide water, install heaters, and build guard towers. I was basically in charge of anything to do with building up the base, and of course all while continuing my primary duties as an infantry man. This was not an easy task, supplies were sparse and working conditions were intense. The guys were counting on me to one day get a shower and maybe even be able to wash some clothes. I was honored to be in charge of this task, and by God's strength I would be able to accomplish what I was assigned to do.

During that first night in my metal box I laid there on my bed, praying about how to start a Bible study. No sooner did I finish praying when I heard a knock on the door of my hooch. The voice said, "Hey it's Brian, do you want to start a Bible study? We are meeting at the supply tent at 1900 hours." I immediately replied "Sure," and was blown away how fast God answered that prayer. This was the beginning of something very special that would change the landscape of the valley and the lives of many soldiers as our deployment went on.

Our first meeting took place in the one tent that was primarily empty except for a few random supplies. Ten soldiers showed up to that first Bible study and it was beautiful. There we all sat in a freezing cold tent with no lights or heat, but it didn't seem to matter. We were in the presence of God's power as we gathered around his Word. We all turned our head lamps on and began reading scripture and talking about how we were all feeling. Hope sprang up in that first study and the unity was remarkable. We had Catholics, Baptists, Southern Baptists, Pentecostals, and Charismatics, all sitting around God's word and drawing comfort from His promises. There were no theological arguments, only unity around God's Word and our common struggle and purpose.

After we finished reading scripture, we all discussed the best way to move forward, since there were so many different denominations represented. We decided that we would not focus on our differences but instead we were going to let the Word of God dictate and unite us. Our differences did not matter, what mattered was Jesus and what God's word said. What happened after that is nothing short of miraculous as we saw the power of God uniting His children through His Word and the Holy Spirit. We also decided that we would meet twice a week and once on Sundays. We did not have a Chaplain out there, so we decided that anyone who wanted to preach could and we would all take turns.

Our study and service began to grow. It went from 10 to 15, and then to 20, and before we knew it there up to 30 soldiers showing up for study and/or service. This would go on for several months. There was so much power there that the Commander took notice and gave us permission to move our study and service to the chow hall so we could have power and heat. I remember the Chaplain coming out to visit for the first time. You could see the look of awe on his face as he sat in our service. God was raising up preachers, teachers, and evangelists in the middle of nowhere on a remote base that was under constant attack from the enemy.

It was a few months into our deployment that I first met two South African Special Forces guys that were assigned to our base to help train Afghan National Security Forces. When I spoke to them about the Bible study, they were both extremely excited. They were Charismatic believers and each had taken part and attended huge revivals in South Africa. One of them told me about a movie called "Faith like Potatoes," which was the story of how a seven year revival began in South Africa. He told me how he went to one of these revivals and how it changed his life forever. I grew close to these two men and they impacted my life greatly. I remember sitting in their hooch one night, speaking to one of them for hours about God and how He works in our lives. When I started this chapter, I told you about the vision I had at 9 years old and how I saw that exact image when I first got off the helicopter. I was nervous and reluctant to share with this man what happened because I did not want him to think I was crazy or making up the story. I finally decided I would share my experience with him. I told him about the vision and how I was convinced it was from God, and that I did not know what it meant or why it happened, but that I simply could not shake it. I also shared with him that about the same time I had another vision. I was sitting in a Christmas Eve service when I had this overwhelming feeling that someday I wanted to talk about God like the man up front did. I told him, "I don't want you to think I am crazy, but I simply can't let these things go." I did not have to wait long for a response. He smiled and said, "That's just God giving you a mile marker." My jaw dropped. He then went on to say, "God just wants you to know He has you right where He wants you!" To describe in words how that impacted me would be almost impossible. The comfort, relief, purpose, and peace I felt was beyond words. I thanked him and told him, "I never thought of it that way." This single conversation changed my perspective on all the losses, struggles, and doubts I was having. It became clear at that moment that God had me there for a reason and it was my job to be obedient to the mission God had given me.

Our Bible study and services continued to thrive, and the Chaplain looked forward to his visits. We overcame our first hurdle when Easter came up. Some of the guys wanted to have a Catholic Chaplain administer the Eucharist, while others looked at the bread and juice as more symbolic and there was no need for a Chaplain to distribute it. There were no arguments, we simply said it's all about Jesus. If some wanted the chaplain to do it then so be it. What was important was not who did it, but that we were bringing God honor and celebrating Christ rising from the dead. Our chapel group was united not through our efforts, but through Christ Himself, so when these differences came up we simply prayed and continued with the mission.

In the Muslim faith they have a call to prayer five times a day. We liked these calls to prayer because we knew that during them we would not be attacked. The most dangerous time was right after because I guess they made their peace with their god and were ready to leave this world to what they were promised in the afterlife. The call to prayer came over a loud speaker that rang through the valley for all to hear. I remember gathering at one of our Bible studies and discussing that we needed to have praise and worship ringing through the valley instead. As God would have it, we had a guy who was gifted in music and even had a guitar. It was decided the next service and every service thereafter would feature praise and worship. I cannot express the joy that was experienced as we began to sing our praises to God. Our studies at that point were held around 20:00 hours or 8pm, so the valley was pitch black and quiet. There was no question in our minds that our praises echoed through that valley and the thought that it was the first time those echoes were heard in that darkness was in itself a beautiful experience. There is no doubt that God was scattering seeds throughout that valley for those that heard it. Perhaps we will see some of those people in heaven as God waters those seeds and makes them grow.

Like a Master weaver, God knits together the events of our lives to create a beautifully patterned fabric. As the author records in Psalm 139:13-17, "For you created my inmost being; you knit me together in my mother's womb. I praise you because I am fearfully and wonderfully made; your works are wonderful, I know that full well. My frame was not hidden from you when I was made in the secret place. When I was woven together in the depths of the earth, your eyes saw my unformed body. All the days ordained for me were written in your book before one of them came to be. How precious to me are your thoughts O God! How vast is the sum of them!"

As we face life with its challenges and obstacles, we can trust that all along God is using these events and circumstances to accomplish an even greater plan which involves conforming us into the image of His Son, all, that our lives would bring Him glory! In Ephesians 2:10 we read, "We are His workmanship created in Christ Jesus unto good works which God prepared beforehand that we should walk in them."

As we seek to follow Him, he will lead us into those works. Each of us has a mission to complete and as we keep our eyes on Him, we can trust that He will enable us to finish and not only to finish, but to finish well.

Dear Lord, I owe you my life and my salvation. Thank you for calling me and preparing work beforehand for me to walk in. I recognize that you knew me intimately, even when I was being formed in my mother's womb. Please forgive me for allowing the distractions of this life to keep me from pursuing you with my whole heart. Use me Lord to glorify yourself.

AAR Reflection:

1. How have your life's experiences prepared you to serve the Lord?

2. Read Ephesians 2:10 once again. How does that give you confidence to keep moving forward?

Chapter 5

"Hey, no fair I wasn't looking!"

Many of us have had near death experiences at some point in our lives, that's not all that unusual. Our responses to these experiences vary and the lasting effects may vary as well. For soldiers, these experiences are commonplace depending on what your job is and where you are serving. I think it is important that you the reader understand that every job in the military is critical to the mission. The title Airborne Infantry (Paratrooper) and other titles like Navy SEAL, Ranger, or Special Forces sound impressive and are certainly the tip of the spear, but they are just the tip. The tip is supported by the rest of the spear and cannot function without it. This is important to understand because whether it's the U.S. Army or God's Army, everyone's job is important to achieve the mission. For example, we could not have functioned if it were not for those men and women who packed up those bottles of water and prepared them for shipping.

After my months of training and preparation for our mission in Afghanistan, reality set in quickly as I realized this was no longer a training exercise. The bullets were real and the enemy really wanted to kill me. It's hard to describe the feeling you get once you realize that you are just a target in your enemy's mind and given the opportunity, they will try to eliminate that target. Now to be fair, the enemy was our target as well. Military training instills a disconnect mentally in soldiers, it has to. When you look down a rifle site, you do not identify what you see as a person, but as a target or a threat. That is just the reality of war, it's not personal it's just war.

My biggest fear, other than experiencing a horrible death, was "freezing up" when the time came. It was explained to us in our training that during a combat situation the normal heart rate of 60 beats per minute can shoot up to 200 beats per minute in a matter of seconds. When the adrenaline rush hits you can "freeze up" and literally not be able to think or act, which renders you combat ineffective.

This has little to do with whether someone has courage or not. It has more to do with how your body is conditioned to handle this dramatic shift. This is why during our training we were screamed at while tired and hungry, and put under constant physical and mental stress. That training would help prepare us for the stress of combat and reduce the odds of "freezing up."

I often asked God to give me the courage to fight well regardless of the outcome when the time came. I did not want to have to live with the knowledge that I froze up and could not perform my mission. I have come to find out that "freezing up" can happen to any soldier at any time. If it does happen, it is not talked about out of respect for the soldier. If it is a normal occurrence for a soldier then command would intervene and deal with that soldier privately.

It was a typical day for me in the Tangi Valley. I had just finished lunch and was heading back to my hooch (Living Quarters). It was early in our deployment, but as the weather got warmer the amount of random gunfire, mortar, and rocket attacks was increasing. This was expected because the Taliban are for the most part "fair weather" fighters. As I was walking back to my hooch I heard gunfire. I immediately stopped and listened. As I listened I was asking myself, "Were these just random shots or was it an outright attack?" My question was answered quickly as the gunfire became more and more rapid. It sounded like it was coming from different locations and was getting louder by the second. My heart started pounding! I ran to my hooch and grabbed my vest, bullets, and helmet. It was game time! Many of the soldiers were sleeping in their racks or just relaxing when it started. I began to sprint towards the sound of the loudest gunfire and as I was running, I was looking for a good fighting position from our outer wall. I finally made it to the wall with another soldier at my side. I immediately started scanning for targets. The gunfire began to slow down and eventually stopped. Within seconds there were 50 more soldiers in fighting positions, waiting and watching. I was scared but was also comforted knowing that we all had each other's backs and were ready for the fight.

This was my first experience charging towards gunfire. As I reflected on my sprint to the wall, I was baffled by what was running through my mind; "This so cool. No it's not, this is crazy!

I can't believe I am running towards bullets! Thank you God for the courage! Could this be my last day on this Earth?" All those thoughts raced through my mind in the seconds it took to get to the wall. Even though I was baffled by my thoughts, I felt a deep sense of joy and satisfaction that when the time came I ran to and not from the fight. To some this may sound silly, but for a soldier it's an accomplishment. I had often prayed for God to remove my fear, but He was teaching me that He was bigger than my fear and would give me the courage I needed for battle. As a soldier I was given a mission, and the mission outweighed my comfort. God was showing me through this experience that the mission He planned for me not only outweighs my comfort, but even my life here on this Earth.

I will never forget the first time I was shot at directly. Unfortunately for me it was not a rifle but a RPG (Rocket Propelled Grenade). I had just finished emailing my wife, and as I took my first couple of steps outside the tent I heard what sounded like an explosion! I quickly realized that it was the sound of an RPG being fired. It's not like the movies where you have time to duck out of the way. You have just a few seconds before it hits the target. In the first milliseconds after I heard it, my first thought was, "Hey! No fair I wasn't looking!" My second thought was, "That was the stupidest last thought on the planet!" I finally decided to duck the best I could in the few seconds I had. As the rocket traveled just above me I heard what sounded like airbrakes.

I could feel the heat from the rocket discharge as it passed by. It was by God's providence that the round was fired from about 400 meters away. The rocket from an RPG starts to travel up after 300 meters because it starts to lose its speed. That rocket ended up missing me and hit the side of a hill about 20 meters away. I know it was God's hand guiding that rocket and keeping me out of harm's way. As I look back I still laugh because I don't think I will ever understand my thought process when confronted with that near-death experience. I think when a person is often exposed to those experiences you become hardened by your new normal. You begin to process these events in ways that most people would not. God was using these events to refine my heart and remind me that the purpose He has for my life is bigger than the intent of the enemy who fired that RPG.

There were several instances where as a soldier I was called to overcome my fear and place everything into God's hands for the sake of the mission. I know those lessons still apply today as I serve Him on the front lines of ministry. During our deployment we had a few National Guard engineers at our base to help build up our infrastructure. I remember when they first arrived, I was standing by one of tents explaining some of the issues we were having with our power supply. We were standing next to the gym tent when suddenly someone in the gym dropped a weight and it made a loud noise. I immediately grabbed my weapon and turned towards the noise. One of the engineers said, "Relax, why are you so jumpy?" I told him "Give it a few days." As fate would have it, about two days later that engineer was working on a project when the first Mortar came in and landed about 10 meters from him. The only thing that saved him was a sand bag wall between him and the blast. They shot a few more that day and followed it up with some small arms fire. At that point we all ran towards the gunfire to our fighting positions. The attack did not amount to much. It was more annoying than anything. However, after the attack was over one of the engineers came up to me and said, "I have never seen anything like that in my life! While I was running for cover you guys were running towards machine gun fire!" Needless to say he never told me to relax again or asked why I was so jumpy.

Life in the Tangi Valley was hostile to say the least, but the peace of God was there amidst that hostility. The mission depended on our willingness to run to battle when called, regardless of the personal sacrifice. During our training before coming to the Tangi our command had one simple order, "Do Not Surrender! If you run out of bullets throw your rifle at them! It is better to meet your maker fighting than to give up!" God was teaching me that personal sacrifice was part of the mission. I only needed to trust God and remain focused on the mission. God would take care of the rest.

As Christians, we are living in enemy territory facing a very real enemy. As the scriptures teach, "For we wrestle not against flesh and blood, but against powers, against rulers of the darkness of this age, against spiritual wickedness in the heavenly places" (Eph 6:12). It is amazing how many of us tend to forget that we are heavenly citizens occupying enemy territory until He comes back. Each of us is called to be sober and vigilant because our adversary, the devil walks about like a roaring lion seeking whom he may devour (1 Pet 5:8). In other words, if we are going to have any chance at success, we as soldiers in God's army, on the front line need to be prepared. We need to be ready for battle at all times.

"We need to take a stand having girded our waist with truth, having put on the breastplate of righteousness, and having our feet shod with the preparation of the gospel of peace; above all taking the shield of faith with which we will be able to quench the fiery darts of the wicked one. And taking the helmet of salvation and the sword of the Spirit, which is the Word of God. Praying always with all prayer and supplication in the Spirit and being watchful to this end with all perseverance and supplication for all the saints." (Eph 6:14-18)

God has given us every weapon we need, both defensively and offensively to accomplish the mission. We need to be ready to run into battle. The enemy has taken too many captives with his lies and schemes. All we need to do is take a good look at the world around us to see that casualties are mounting up. Addictions, abuses, murder, hatred, hopelessness and despair. We have been called as well as charged to take back ground the enemy has taken. The glorious gospel message brings hope to the hopeless, freedom to the captives and sight to those who have been blinded. Are you willing to run headfirst into enemy fire or are you going to look around to take cover? Consider this your call to action, your call to battle... your call to surrender!

Dear Lord help me this day to lean and trust completely in you. Enable me to run headfirst into battle. Help me to take up the whole armor of God that I may withstand the assaults of the evil one. When the enemy throws his fiery darts, may I take up the shield of faith with which to quench them. May I also remember to take the helmet of salvation and the sword of the Spirit which is your Word dear God. And may I always go prepared to share Your mighty Gospel of peace. Give me the courage and boldness to declare your glorious message of hope to a world that is lost and dying.

AAR Reflections:

1. How have you responded to the battle call of evangelism? Do you seek to be a witness or do you seek to take cover?

2. What prevents you from sharing your faith with others? From running toward the battle?

Chapter 6

"Mortar Fridays"

It's most likely one of the most popular sayings in our society as the weekend draws near, "Thank God it's Friday" or "TGIF." This statement usually signals the end of a long hard week at work. Most people on Fridays are planning their weekend or checking their honey do lists. However, in the Tangi Valley, Fridays were viewed very differently. In our world Friday often signaled Mortar or rocket attacks from the enemy. Between mortars, RPG's, and large rockets, our Combat Outpost took well over 100 rounds during our year stay. Often these attacks were ineffective, meaning we did not sustain damage to life or serious damage to our infrastructure. Don't get me wrong, many of those projectiles landed inside the walls of our base and most were within a 100 to 150 meters from their intended target. Even so, this was way too close for comfort. We often laughed about how bad their aim was, but in the back of our minds we knew that at some point they would not miss. Joking was our way of dealing with the everyday stress of being a target. It was in the midst of this that God's hand of protection became evident to me as He showed me that He alone was our greatest defense.

As our deployment moved on, in time, the attacks began to change. We started to notice they were happening more on Fridays, and they were becoming increasingly more accurate. I think it is important to explain that contrary to what is depicted in Hollywood movies, a mortar round does not whistle on the way in before it lands. When a mortar attack happens the first thing you hear is the explosion, there is no warning. It's hard to describe the feeling of going about your daily routine and in an instant, upon the sound of that explosion you try to gather your thoughts and prepare for battle. My mind would instantly begin to race and I would try to process what my next move was, knowing that once that first mortar came in, more would be and I only had a minute or so to find cover. Its then that your ears tune in and you listen for the faint thump in the distance which is the sound of another mortar being fired. At that point you know you have about 30 seconds before that round lands and all you can do is pray it does not land on you or on your buddies.

We nicknamed these days "Mortar Fridays." Our intelligence people informed us that the Taliban acquired a guy who knew how to fire mortars and that his aim was spot on. Apparently, he fought the Russians when they invaded Afghanistan back in 1979, and the Taliban rotated him around the country to attack different bases. On Thursdays he fired on a base in Logar Province. It became clear to us from the increasing accuracy of the attacks that he was scheduled to fire at us on Fridays. It was also evident that he knew how to fire a mortar and how to hit his target. As Mortar Fridays went on, many of our structures started to get hit. Though most attacks happened at about 1 pm, we started seeing the attacks come at more random times.

One attack in particular was probably one of the most terrifying experiences during my deployment in Afghanistan and still haunts me to this day. It occurred in the morning which was very unusual. I was sound asleep in my bunk when I heard a loud explosion. It was so close I felt the over pressure from the blast. I shot up out of my bunk from a deep sleep, startled, confused, scared, and disoriented. I tried a to gather my thoughts enough to grab my weapon and gear. I knew I only had a minute or so until another round would be coming. I stumbled out of my hooch, still half asleep and tried to find cover and figure out what was going on. I can tell you this was not a good way to wake up. Because of this event, a fear of falling asleep was implanted in my mind, resulting in many sleepless nights which continue even until now. Two more rounds came in that morning and we started to think that maybe they were going to try to overrun our base. I cannot explain how the combination of fear, sleepiness, confusion, and trying to remain focused on preparing for an attack felt or why it still haunts me to this day, but it does.

One Friday shortly after we completed building our Chapel, I was with one of my commanding officers on the Afghan army side of our outpost. As we spoke with the Afghan army an explosion happened about 25 meters from our location striking one of our living quarters with a direct hit. We looked at each other for a second and then began running to our side of the base. Thankfully there was only a couple soldiers in the structure that got hit and none were seriously injured. As we reached our side and rounded the corner to take cover, a second mortar came in and landed within feet of the first one. The impact position was so close that we felt the heat and over blast pressure as the round exploded. One soldier who was standing just a couple of feet from us was hit with shrapnel but miraculously was not seriously injured.   After the second explosion, myself and about 20 or so soldiers were hunkered down in our makeshift bunker by 2nd platoons living quarters. We heard the distant thump and knew round number three was coming. It landed about 15 meters from our position. The level of fear began to rise because we recognized this attack was effective and accurate. We listened and waited and about a minute later we heard another thump in the distance and we all knew what that meant. I was on the left side of the bunker when I looked over at a young soldier. I saw the fear in his eyes and noted that he was visibly shaken, so I said to him, "It's going to be alright," no sooner did those words come out of my mouth when the mortar came in and hit the left side of our bunker. Dirt and dust fell on us and it was as if time stood still as we waited for the BOOM. That day we took 13 mortar rounds that damaged almost all our structures and much of our equipment. All the rounds were on target but as God would have it, there was only one DUD round of the day, the one that hit our bunker dead on. About 18 inches of dirt were between us and that mortar round. Had it exploded we surely would have sustained casualties. My first thought when the blast did not come was a passage from the Book of Romans, "Therefore if God is for us who can be against us." It was the hand of God that protected us that day, and just for the record, most of the soldiers in that bunker were attending chapel. One currently pastors a church. It was then I realized they cannot build a bomb powerful enough to thwart the plan that God has for your life.

There were several more attacks on our base and our enemy relentlessly tried many different tactics to destroy us. Thankfully God's protection and blessing were upon us. Another thing I recall, was that my fellow soldiers and I used to sit by the chow hall and watch helicopters fly in and out. It was well known by us and even the pilots that flying in low from the south was never a good idea. Even though we warned pilots and they were aware of this, they continued to fly into our outpost low and from the south. When we heard the sound of the helicopters coming we would sit by the chow hall and just wait. We waited for the sound of an RPG being fired or for the sound of gunfire. Many times as we sat and waited the inevitable would happen, the helicopter would be fired upon. Thankfully they were not accurate shots so we did not lose any helicopters. To this day I still do not understand why they continued to fly in from that direction.

There was nothing more frightening than flying into our combat post, especially since they always flew in from the south. Unfortunately, I had to do it several since I was in charge of getting the supplies we needed to build up our Combat Outpost. Most of the time I flew on non-military helicopters flown by the lowest bidder who apparently were drunk Russian pilots. I remember getting into a helicopter and it was evident this Russian pilot had been drinking. As I was sitting in the helicopter preparing to take off I felt a drip on the back of my neck. I shouted to the pilot, "Something is leaking!" He said in a thick Russian accent "It's just a little hydraulic fluid, it's fine!" Not an encouraging or comforting statement to hear before take-off. It was by God's grace that I arrived at FOB (Forward Operating Base) Schank safely. I was only at FOB Schank for two days and was able to complete my mission and gather the supplies we needed. Once that was complete it was time for my return flight to the Tangi Valley. I have to say I was very unsettled because I knew flying back was dangerous, especially if they came in from the south. I also knew that there would be a group of soldiers at the outpost sitting by the chow hall watching and waiting as I had done many times.

I boarded the helicopter and it was the same helicopter along with the same drunk Russian pilot. As we approached the Tangi I shouted to the pilot, "Don't fly in low from the south!" He did not respond and continued his approach. I began praying that we would land without incident. For some reason getting shot at on the ground just seemed safer than when you were in a helicopter. Sure enough about a minute from landing I felt two hard thumps right below my feet! We were taking hits from small arms fire and had taken two rounds to the bottom of the helicopter. The pilot quickly dipped hard to the right. Thankfully the rounds did not penetrate the floor or damage the helicopter and we were able to land safely.

God was teaching me to rest in His protection and His plan. I was being shown that His plans are greater than man's. This is not to say that I was not scared or shaken during these events, but as my time in the Tangi pressed on, I was drawing closer to God and depending more on His Armor and Protection than my own. God was preparing me for the fiery darts that Satan would use to attack me and was also building my trust in His protection and in His armor.

The Christian walk is filled with obstacles and trials, some of our own making and others through no fault of our own. As Christians, we have an enemy and he is cunning and fierce. His assaults can be relentless and accurate. With that in mind, I would like to borrow a powerful phrase from the scriptures, "But God," "But God," "But God." You see, we are not left out on our own. We have a God, a most powerful, loving God who is for us. Knowing this to be the case, "If God is for us, who can be against us?" We can walk in this life with great confidence and assert as the Prophet wrote of Israel in Isaiah 54:17, "No weapon formed against you shall prosper, and every tongue which rises against you in judgement you shall condemn. This is the heritage of the servants of the Lord, and their righteousness is from Me, says the Lord."

Dear Lord, when I feel like fainting under my circumstances, help me to lean on you. When I am worried for the future, help me to remember that you are in control. Father, go before me and make me the vessel you need me to be, that I would bring you honor and glory. I confess that I am weak, but I know that you are strong. Thank you for your precious word that reminds me that if you are for me, who can be against me.

AAR Reflections:

1. How big is your view of God? When faced with life's challenges, do you believe that God is enough? If not, why?

2. In what areas have you let fear and doubt replace peace and faith in your life?

Chapter 7

"Pray for Angels at our Corners"

As my deployment neared the halfway point, I began counting the months and even weeks until I would ship out. As a result, tensions began to rise as we all hoped to make it home in one piece. Plans for pulling out and heading home were starting to ramp up. We started shipping equipment and even some supplies back to Italy in late August. Command teams from the unit replacing us began to arrive for brief periods to see what they were in for and check the status of our infrastructure. We had made some huge strides during our time there. We actually had working showers, however the water supply was still contaminated with sewage from Kabul which was upstream from where we drew our water. I had built a small laundry facility so washing clothes was now possible, provided we had the water. Trailer type buildings were beginning to be shipped in to replace the tents we had been living in for the past year. We had heat in most areas and even air conditioning in some of our living spaces. As far as the base improvements and living conditions went, the mission was a success.

However, as our time there was drawing to a close, the valley was more active than ever. The insurgents were not on our schedule to leave and they did not lay off their attempts to cause as much damage and as many casualties as possible. Mortar and rocket attacks truly became the norm for our last few months and the stress levels began rising among the soldiers. Being so close to going home and knowing the attacks were increasing loomed heavily on our minds. Too many stories had been told of guys dying just days or even hours before they shipped out to go home. And while no one wants to die, it just seemed like it would somehow be worse the closer you were to leaving. We had all been through so much and in those final months we all began to grow battle weary. I have already described to you "Mortar Fridays" in the previous chapter, but they began to spread throughout the week and our attacks grew more and more unpredictable and accurate.

A couple of months before we were scheduled to ship out, the Afghan elections were scheduled. Our unit was ordered to send a platoon to help secure the election facilities. They would be picked up and flown to their location by two Chinook Helicopters. The mission was scheduled to take three days. We heard the sound of the Helicopters flying in and 3rd platoon was waiting with their gear on the landing zone so they could board and get out as quickly as possible. We watched them flying in low from the south over the village and we waited anxiously, hoping they would come in without incident. Everything seemed to be going just as planned until they were about 10 feet from the ground. We heard the initiation but this time it was not an RPG but a 107mm rocket which packed a huge punch. We all just froze as we heard that ominous hum. The rocket missed the helicopter by a matter of feet. We know this because Chinooks are equipped with flares that fire automatically from the rear when a rocket comes within close proximity. The flare shot out and landed just a few feet from our fuel depot. The rocket ended up hitting the hill just outside our base. I don't know what was scarier the rocket coming that close or the fact that 3rd platoon still had to board the helicopter and head out for the mission. Praise God they took off without incident.

Yes, as I stated the stress was rising on our base, but so was the power of God through our Bible study. The chaplain stopped his visits due to the frequency of the attacks on our base. This did not stop the plan God had for what He wanted to accomplish on that outpost in the middle of the Tangi Valley. Our commander had given us approval a few months before to move our Bible study from the supply tent to the chow hall because he could see the positive impact of our study on his soldiers. He was truly inspired by what was happening and how our Bible study went from a few soldiers to over 30 and was now called the "Tangi Christian Fellowship.". We started talking about how awesome it would be to build a Chapel. It would be our altar to the Lord and a symbol of what God had accomplished in this remote valley. Through prayer and the power of God, it was decided I would be given the mission to ask the commander if we could use some scrap wood and materials to build a chapel. As I was talking with my commander he began to smile and said, "Absolutely!" God had answered our prayers and made it possible to build our Altar to the Lord in the Tangi! When I told the guys, we were all so excited because we knew this was a mission God had given us. We started making plans to build what we would later name the Tangi Chapel. It is important to mention here that we all knew that building this chapel would come with consequences from the enemy which loomed outside our walls. The chapel was certain to bring more attacks because, as we know, the darkness hates the light and God was allowing us to shine His light in that valley.

We decided to put a steeple on our chapel that was high enough to see from outside the walls. On top would sit a cross made of iron for all to see. We gathered up our scrap wood and began building the Tangi Chapel. I think it took less than a week to build because we were all so excited and honored to be used by God. The completed chapel was equipped with small pews, heat, and a pulpit in the front with a cross on the front of it made entirely of nails.

I will never forget that little chapel and the hope it brought to us all. According to our commander and Chaplain, it was the first soldier initiated chapel ever built on a combat outpost. We were all so encouraged knowing that not only would praise and worship be heard throughout the valley, but now the Cross of Jesus Christ would stand tall for all to see! Amen.

As I stated earlier, it came with consequences from our enemy. They were not too happy with our chapel or the fact that no matter how many times they attacked, their weapons were ineffective. Our Chapel and steeple would become a target for the enemy, but even when the rockets came in, only minor damage occurred with only minor injuries to our soldiers. Talk about God's power and His protection! I can only imagine their frustration knowing regardless of what they tried, our chapel service continued as did our praise and worship.

One chapel service stood out to me. That day we were attacked, and our outpost took direct hits from several mortars. As we all showed up for chapel service that night there was a battle weary quietness among us. Our faith was being tested and our hearts were growing weary as time went on and the attacks continued.

While we were sitting in the chapel talking about the day, and how we were all battle weary, one of our South African friends who was on guard duty came running into the chapel. We all just looked at him and waited to hear some bad news. He said "I was sitting in the guard tower when God put on my heart to tell you guys this story!"

"There was a husband leaving for a long trip and he would be leaving his wife and children behind. Before he left he said we need to pray for Angels at our four Corners which they did. As fate would have it, four men were waiting for him to leave and planned on killing his family shortly after he left. A few hours later, the wife got a knock on the door from some soldiers and they had four men with them. The four men were visibly shaken and turned themselves in to the authorities. The men explained that just as they were preparing to make their attack they saw four giant beings on the four corners of the house and immediately knew God was guarding this house!"

He then said, "God put it on my heart to tell you guys that story." And then he left. We all sat there for a minute and after a brief silence we agreed we should pray for God's Angels at our four corners which we did. Our study went from somber to joyful, realizing that God truly had our backs and was protecting and blessing us.

The day was drawing near for me to leave COP Tangi but not before God again would reassure me that He was in control the whole time. I was doing a walkthrough with a soldier from the unit relieving us. I was showing him the outpost and the current infrastructure. As I was walking another soldier from the new unit came up to me out of nowhere and asked me, "Were you a part of building that chapel?" I answered and said "Yes." He said "You are not going to believe this, but I came to know the Lord two weeks before I left for Afghanistan. One of my wife's biggest concerns was how was I going to attend church. I could not believe my eyes when I flew in and as I looked out of the helicopter the first thing I saw was the steeple with the Cross on it!"

I smiled and said "I guess we built it for you then. Take good care of it for us." I think God likes to show off sometimes and just flex a little to remind us of who He is.

The day to leave finally arrived. It was about 2 am and we were waiting for our flight to make our way home. I sat in that Chapel one last time and prayed and thanked God for all He had done and all He had taught me over the last year. Then I prayed one of those silly prayers. I asked God if there were Angels at our four corners, to make it known to me. I know what some of you might be thinking, because I was thinking it myself, but I figured I would try anyway. As I stepped out of the chapel one final time, I took one last look and thought to myself "This is the most beautiful chapel I have ever seen." Then I went to the landing zone and waited for the Chinooks to come in and pick us up.

It was a perfectly clear night and it was bitter cold. As our group of soldiers waited, most attendees of the chapel were standing there when the sky lit up with the brightest light any of us had ever seen. We waited for the sound of thunder or a boom but heard nothing. We all wondered what that was, but our minds quickly shifted focus as the helicopters approached. We gathered all our stuff, got on the helicopter and took off. Then it hit me! God gave me the sign I had prayed for just moments before. That flash of light was God letting me know He had our four corners! I smiled and kept that one to myself.

The unit before we arrived in the Tangi Valley had lost four soldiers and over twenty injured. The unit that came in after us lost over ten soldiers within the three months they stayed in the Tangi before turning the base over to the Afghan Army. In August of 2011, thirty-nine soldiers lost their lives when a Chinook helicopter was shot down in the Tangi Valley. Most of those killed were Navy SEALs. Our unit spent a year in the Tangi Valley and by God's mercy and grace we only had three soldiers seriously injured, and they all made full recoveries. We did not lose a single soldier in that valley. God certainly had His mighty hand of protection over us that year and He changed our lives forever in the process.

In Psalm 91 we read, "He who dwells in the secret place of the Most High shall abide under the shadow of the Almighty. I will say of the Lord, 'He is my refuge and my fortress; My God, in Him will I trust.' Surely He will deliver you from the snare of the fowler and from the perilous pestilence. He shall cover you with His feathers, and under His wings you shall take refuge; His truth shall be your shield and buckler. You shall not be afraid of the terror by night, Nor of the arrow that flies by day, nor of the pestilence that walks in darkness, nor of the destruction that lays waste at noonday. A thousand may fall at your side, and ten thousand at your right hand; but it shall not come near you. Only with your eyes shall you look and see the reward of the wicked. Because you have made the Lord, who is my refuge, even the Most

High, your dwelling place, no evil shall befall you, nor shall any plague come near your dwelling; For He shall give angels charge over you, to keep you in all your ways..."

In verse one, the word dwell means to remain in, or to abide in. Now, please understand that this is different from just visiting His secret place. This Psalm is referring to the one who makes it his pursuit to abide in the shadow of the Almighty. God promises this person His protection. This is a beautiful picture of the Father's care and protection for His children who have committed themselves to His pursuit. When we are serving the King of Kings and the Lord of Lords, we can proceed with confidence and without fear. If He has charged us with a mission, we can be assured that He will see that we complete it, if we keep our eyes on Him. At times we may grow tired and weary, but in the secret place of the Most High we will find rest and strength to continue. God has never promised us that the Christian walk would be easy, but He does promise to walk alongside us throughout the entire journey.

I would like to illustrate this by recounting an event in the life of Charles Spurgeon, an influential turn of the century preacher. He stated that in 1854, the neighborhood in London where he served was visited by Asiatic Cholera and many in his congregation were taken ill. Every day he was called to visit the sick and bury the dead to the extent that he became weary in body and sick at heart. One day he was returning mournfully from a funeral when he was led to read a newspaper hanging up in a shoemaker's window. Standing out in bold print he read, "Because you have made the Lord, which is my refuge, even the Most High, your habitation; there shall no evil befall you, nor shall any plague come near your dwelling." He then went on with renewed strength and faith to comfort those in need and carry out the mission God had given him.

Oh Most High God, help me to dwell in your secret place that I may be able to claim you as my refuge. Forgive me of the times that I have taken my eyes off you to pursue my own desires. My heart cries out to you this day. My longing is to serve you with all my heart. Father help me to be faithful to your call this day. Amen.

AAR Reflection:

1. What does it mean to abide under the shadow of the Almighty?

2. In what ways have you made God your refuge?

Chapter 8

"This is going to hurt!"

My deployment was over and by God's grace, mercy and protection, our entire company 1/503 M.O.D. (March or Die) 173rd Airborne Combat Team was reunited with their families. I have said many times in this book thus far that it is hard to put into words some of the feelings and events that took place during our deployment. Coming home and being reunited with your family is one of those events. It's pure excitement, joy, and happiness. Seeing your family for the first time in months, knowing you made it out in one piece is just one of those moments you never forget.

After landing in Italy we made our way back to our base on Coach busses. We were crammed in the bus and as usual there was not enough room for everyone and all our stuff, but who cared! We were going home. As we approached the base we started to see the "Welcome Home!" signs strewn along the entrance to our base. Balloons were whipping in the wind and my heart began to pound faster and faster. As we pulled up to the gym and stepped off the bus I could hear the cheering coming from inside as soldiers began making their way in. As I stepped into the gym I was overwhelmed. The cheering and hugs were unbelievable. I searched frantically for my family in a sea of hundreds of joy-filled people. Then it happened! There they were. As I stated earlier, the words to describe that feeling simply would not and could not do it justice. What surprised me was that in the midst of all that joy were seeds of fear. "What do I say? Do I seem happy enough? Are they happy? Has war changed me? Can I adapt to being home?" while these thoughts did not trump my happiness they were still there. My wife and children looked beautiful and embracing them brought me a deep sense of peace.

Many have heard the saying "You may leave the war, but the war never leaves you." There is a lot of truth to that statement. I think many people who have never experienced what combat veterans have often use the worst case scenarios they read or hear about when it comes to this topic. A small majority of veterans come back and truly never adapt back into civilian life and become unable to function as employees, spouses, parents, and members of society. This is, however, a very small percentage. Most combat veterans successfully integrate back into civilian life and achieve great things and are productive members of society. That all being said, you are forever changed after experiencing war and prolonged separation from your family. The lens you see life through changes dramatically. There is a disconnect that war instills in a person, that during the stress of combat is a survival tactic, but in society and family life can appear cold and distant and at times even be an obstacle.

Part of our re-integration training was to meet with an Army psychologist to make sure we were adjusting to our family and home life well. They were also checking to make sure we were not a danger to ourselves or anyone around us. As we have all read and heard, the suicide rates for returning veterans is extremely high. I remember sitting in the room with this psychologist and him asking the question, "So tell me about the last three years of your life?" I thought to myself "Really?" As I sat there baffled by the question, he asked it again. I thought for a minute and then said "OK, you want to know about the last three years of my life." "Yes" he replied.

I took a deep breath and answered "In 2008 my business partner robbed our company about $200,000 which began my financial death spiral. Then in August of 2008 I lost my mom, my business shut down, the bank was going to foreclose on our house, and I was dead broke with a wife and three children. I decided at that point to join the military at 37 years old to make sure my family was provided for and because, quite frankly, I just wanted to get away from all the chaos. As funny as this might sound to you doc, the Army seemed like a much needed break at that point."

He shook his head and started writing. I continued. "After joining the Army I found out I was going to be stationed in Italy and that my wife and two of my children would be coming. In addition, I would have to move five thousand miles away from my son John who was living with my ex-wife. When I got to Italy my family was delayed because their passports had been stolen. I was afraid because I knew we were to be deploying in a few months and if they did not get out here within a couple months of the deployment the Army might not let them come and they would have nowhere to live"

He stopped writing and was just looking at me intently so I continued on. "Then I left for deployment to the Tangi Valley which, as you know, is not a very nice place. Halfway through my deployment my father passed away and my brother decided to steal as much money as he could from him. During my 14 day leave, while being excited to see my family, I also had to make arrangements for my father's funeral and take care of his house and finances. Then I left to go back to the Tangi and by God's Grace made it home and here I sit with you today."

He looked at me and started to shake his head and said, "Any one of the things you mentioned even by itself is a major life stressor." He then asked with a puzzled look on his face "How are you functioning so well and how did you get through all that?"

I smiled and said, "Through faith in Jesus Christ. I would not be sitting here without Him." Apparently, I passed the exam because I was allowed to take my leave.

As expected during deployment, you grow close to those you serve alongside. It's not just the soldiers that develop these special bonds, it's also the spouses we leave behind. While you are gone they begin depending on each other and look to each other for support. It's not just the soldier that sacrifices, it is the family too, and all too often they are forgotten about. They live with the daily possibility that a military car will pull up to the house and a couple soldiers in dress uniforms will come to the door to say your soldier is not coming home. As God would have it my wife became friendly with our neighbor two doors down who just happened to be the wife of one of the guys that helped start and build the chapel in Afghanistan.

We were back for a few months and my neighbor's wife (who I will call Michelle) was about 4 months pregnant. We were struggling to get comfortable at the base chapel and really were not getting much out of it. I was speaking with my neighbor (who I will call Donnie), who at this point was a fellow servant of Christ. He was struggling with the base chapel as well. There was only one other place you could go to church that spoke English. It was an Independent Baptist Church that was started by a Retired Navy SEAL. While he was a great man, I just did not feel at home there and neither did my family or Donnie's family. I would speak to Donnie often and we would reflect on how God united the Tangi Chapel members and how we both yearned for that unity again.

My wife and I were home one night and she said, "I would really like to bring Donnie and his family a meal because they have two other children to feed and Michelle is having a tough time with her pregnancy." I agreed and thought that was a great idea. I cannot remember if we invited them over or went to their house the first time, but either way it was the start of God raising up His servants in our little base community. My wife also mentioned, "Why don't we have a Bible Study when we get together. That would be nice" I would like to take credit for having that idea but my wife would never let me live it down if I tried.

So, we decided that once a week our families would get together for dinner and a Bible study. God was at work behind the scenes, He preparing for His harvest. We decided to invite another family to our Bible study. God was blessing our time together. Donnie and I would take turns leading the study each week. The study continued to grow one family at a time over the next couple of months. It was going so well that we decided to start a Sunday service at our homes. We would rotate houses and preaching between myself and Donnie. What happened after that is nothing short of the Hand of God shining His light in our little base community. Our study grew and at one point I think we were up to over 20 to 30 people coming to the study. I later found out through Donnie that the little study was still going strong over a year after we left Italy and even the Chaplains were attending. It was great to hear that they were baptizing people and that the Light of the Gospel would far exceed my stay in that little base community.

My Army career was moving along and it was time to decide whether we were going to stay in the military or not. I was within 14 months of my current contract ending. My Commander sent me to Non-commissioned Officer training school in April after I returned from Afghanistan, which meant I could be promoted to

Sergeant once I completed the school. My wife and I decided to stay in the military because honestly, we had nothing to go back to. Our home was gone, I did not have a job, and we liked the security of the military life.

God again would intervene in my life and take my intentions and throw them in the trash can of my grand plans. I think at this point that trash can was getting a bit full, but I guess I am a little thick headed. While I was in NCO training I was searching an Army website to see if I could change my Army job from Infantry to something else. I was interested in the Psychological Operations jobs, and because I was Airborne Qualified and had my jump wings, I was eligible to join the Special Operations unit that did Psychological Warfare. I started filling out my application for this job, so I could then start the approval process and continue on with my plan of comfort and security. It was halfway through the NCO training when I received an email from the pastor of the church I attended and served at before I joined the military. I had stayed in contact with him over the last couple of years and updated him on what God was doing in my life. As I opened the email and began to read it, I was in shock. He asked, since my tour of duty was almost up if I would be interested in coming back to the church. He offered to let us stay at the parsonage rent free, so long as I went to Bible school and helped him out at the church. Again, I was in total shock for two reasons; first that was not part of my plan; second, I was honored that he asked if I would do that. I immediately called my wife and told her what had happened. She was excited, but I think skeptical at first. We prayed about it and I discussed it with Donnie. Since I had already started the process of re-enlisting and the parsonage was being used at the time for ministry, my wife and I decided that it may not be a good idea.

I remained in contact with the pastor and our "friends" at the church. We planned a trip to come back and visit and decided we would tell the pastor face to face that we would be respectfully declining his invitation. My wife and I felt it may interrupt the ministry at the parsonage so we made our decision to stay in the military. When we arrived back I met with one of the deacons who ran the ministry at the parsonage and he was thrilled with the idea of us coming back and maybe even helping with the ministry. I also spoke to one of the pastors, Mike Tapia, about the idea of coming back. Strangely enough the pastor who invited me back was not available to meet during our weeklong visit. After meeting with Pastor Tapia and speaking more with the Deacon that ran the ministry at the parsonage, my wife and I decided that maybe God was calling us back here after all. We told them we had to pray about it but would let them know our decision very soon.

When we returned to Italy it became clear that going back was what God wanted us to do. As fate would have it, my application for the Special Operations unit was sent to the wrong email, so I missed the cutoff date and could no longer apply. God was shutting the door on my aspirations of doing my twenty years in the military and serving Him on my terms.

What was interesting at this point is we were thankfully unaware of all the division and discourse going on at the church we were going back to. I remember receiving an email from a member asking me how much my housing stipend would be if I used the Army GI Bill to go to school and if I thought it was a good idea to come back.

I explained to her my arrangement was between leadership and God and politely told her it was none of her business. I got one more email from a close friend of ours who had left the church right before we left for the military. She urged me not to go back because the church was not what it used to be and there were several problems. I responded back to her and said, "At this point I do not think God is calling me there because it will be easy, but because He wants to use me to make a difference." I did not know then how true that statement was until we actually went back and saw all the discourse that was going on.

I guess God knew I was not done wrestling with Him on how I believed my life should go. As our time in the military began to draw to an end, I began to have doubts about our decision and honestly still had my mind focused on the things of this world and how I was going to provide for my family. I was encouraged because I thought, finally, I would be doing what I was called to do and be an assistant to the pastor at our church back in New Jersey after completing Seminary. I was excited and could not wait to see all those "friends" we had left behind. I came up with what I thought was a great Idea and I thought I could "kill two birds with one stone." Since I was not staying on active duty I decided I could join the Army Reserves just in case things did not work out with this whole church deal in New Jersey. I am convinced of this, as sinful beings we are experts at hiding bad motives with noble deeds. Fortunately for us, God knows our hearts and corrects us when need be.

I told my wife my great idea and she went along with it and said, "Go for it." I have to say she is the greatest woman on the planet. She has literally followed me and my "great ideas" around the world and been at my side the entire time. My wife is truly a gift from God and the strongest woman I have ever met. After getting her go ahead, I went to the Reserve recruiter on the base in Italy and signed up for a Special Operations Psychological Unit in New Jersey. This seemed great. I got what I wanted and God got what he wanted. It was perfect. Things were coming together.

It was October 5, 2011, two days after I signed up for the Army Reserve Unit which was my backup plan if the church thing did not work out. It was also about six months before my contract would be complete and I would be returning to New Jersey. In the Military it makes no difference if you are getting out or not, you continue to train and remain combat ready until the day you leave the military and become a civilian.

Our training exercise would be a 30-day field mission in which we would secure an airport from enemy insurgents so supplies and manpower could be flown in. As a paratrooper this would be a common mission to insert ourselves behind enemy lines and secure airfields or disrupt the enemy's ability to move supplies. Our mission would start in Italy and we would fly over the drop zone in Germany, perform a combat jump and begin our exercise. I think it is important that you as the reader understand at this point what a combat jump consists of and how demanding it is on a Paratrooper.

There are basically two types of jumps, one is called a "Hollywood Jump" and the other is called a "Combat Jump." The differences are huge to say the least. During a "Hollywood Jump" you are not required to jump with any gear other than your parachute and helmet. Everyone loves these because it's really nothing more than jumping out of the plane. A "Combat Jump" is a different story altogether. During preparation for a "combat Jump" you pack everything needed for the mission in your Ruck Sack to include clothes, food, batteries, extra ammunition, and whatever else you need, which depends on the length and type of mission. You also jump with your weapon and a full combat load of ammunition which is attached to your bulletproof vest or "Kit" as we would call it. So, to give you an idea, you are usually jumping with close to 200 pounds of gear including your parachute and reserve chute. In order to jump with all your gear, you have to be "rigged" up as we would call it a few hours prior to the jump.

Your Ruck Sack gets attached to your parachute harness at the waist line with what is called a lowering line. The Ruck Sack hangs from the waist down in front of you. Imagine trying to walk with your pants around your ankles and those pants weigh over 100 pounds, that's pretty much what it was like. Your weapon goes in a case at your side, you are wearing your helmet, main parachute on your back, and the reserve chute at your waistline just above your Ruck Sack. Are you starting to get the picture? It's extremely uncomfortable and tiresome to say the least. Many times, when fully "Rigged" a paratrooper cannot even stand up without help. You are like a turtle with a 200-pound shell.

It was 0330 on October 5th , 2011 and it was time to get rigged up. I was tasked with jumping with the extra radio batteries which were extremely heavy. If I remember correctly, my Ruck Sack alone was about 120 pounds. After we all got "rigged" up, the plan was to board C-130s at 0500 and arrive at the Drop Zone by 0600 and begin our mission. That day, 1,100 Paratroopers would jump over the period of a few hours and take part in the mission.

There is one thing you learn about the military very quickly, nothing, and I mean nothing, goes as planned. I stumbled on the first aircraft at about 0500 as expected. Just getting on the aircraft was exhausting, never mind jumping out. Apparently, there was an issue with either the aircraft or the weather in Germany. I will not bore you with too many details, I will just tell you that we flew to Germany and then back to Italy on at least three different aircraft that day. I finally boarded the aircraft I would jump out of at 1700 that evening. I was rigged up for over 12 hours and was exhausted to say the least. I remember thinking to myself, *I am jumping out of this plane with or without a parachute, I don't care. I have got to get out of this gear!* All I will say is, be careful what you wish for.

As I sat on the Aircraft and we arrived at the drop zone, the light inside went from red to green which means it's time to jump. Keep in mind, depending how large the drop zone is you only have about 30 seconds to get 15 Paratroopers out of each side before you pass it. It was my time. I struggled to stand up, I was number 7 or 8 in line to jump out of the door. As the line began moving and soldiers began jumping, I struggled to get to the door out of pure exhaustion. I was on the last aircraft of the day so most of the paratroopers I jumped with were only "rigged" for about 3 hours not over 12 hours. As I jumped out of the plane I did not have enough energy to get a good exit and I ended up tumbling head over heels as I began my decent. My parachute finally opened, and I grabbed my risers and prepared to land in about 25 seconds or so. We are trained to look up to make sure we have a fully opened chute right after it opens. We are also trained to gauge our rate of decent by other paratroopers who jumped the same time to make sure we are not falling too fast and our parachute is working properly. I quickly realized something was wrong. My parachute, while open, seemed to be tangled so my rate of decent was faster than the others. Basically, we call it "burning in." My training kicked in. You only have a matter of seconds to correct the issue otherwise you will hit the ground hard and fast, potentially breaking bones, or worse. I immediately pulled the lowering line attachment so my Ruck Sack would drop from my body and I could pull my reserve parachute. When your Ruck Sack drops it is still attached to you with the lowering line which is about 20 feet long. They do this so you and your gear do not get separated. It would be impossible to land with your Ruck Sack attached to your legs. As my 120-pound Ruck Sack fell that 20 feet, the weight and jerk of it dropping disconnected my left leg harness and the left attachment for my reserve parachute. So, let me put this in simple terms, I was going to "Burn in" and there was nothing I could do about it. I remember thinking to myself, *This is gonna hurt.* no sooner did I think that then I hit the ground so hard I felt my insides slosh up and down in my body. I laid there looking up for a minute and said "Ouch." I could not believe I was alive! God is so good! As I laid there and tried to assess my condition, it was apparent after trying several times that I could not get up. It was then that a gust of wind came which would have been fine except I forgot to undo one of the shoulder latches that connected the parachute to my body, which means I started to get dragged across the drop zone. My first thought was, "Really God, are you serious right now!" I quickly disconnected my shoulder latch and waited for the medics to come. My nickname at work became "Lawn Dart." I guess it fits.

I ended up injuring my back, hip, shoulder, pelvis, neck, and had contusions on some of my organs. Thankfully, other than some random pains I get around pretty well and am able to function normally, considering my injuries. I don't share this with you for the "WOW" factor, I share this because God again in His love and mercy had other plans for my life. God would not allow me to install what I will call a "trap door," a way out of accomplishing what He wanted me to accomplish. As I have stated, God would use me how He saw fit, not how I wanted to be used. He wanted me to trust His plan and not try to set up a backup plan. He is truly a Good, Good Father. I can't help but think of how Jacob wrestled with God and how God touched his hip to serve as a reminder of the encounter. I have some reminders of my own wrestling match and I have to report that He won and is still winning.

Our life on this earth involves a series of events that either draw us closer to God or drive us further apart. Oftentimes we find ourselves questioning the path we find ourselves on. If we are sincere in our seeking for God and His will, the scriptures have a source of encouragement for us in Proverbs 16:9. "A man's heart plans his way, But the LORD directs his steps."

Here the emphasis is on the Lord. Though we may think a certain plan is best suited to accomplish the goal, it is the Lord, as we rely and lean on Him, that directs the outcome. What is truly amazing is that not one of our experiences are ever wasted in God's economy. The ups and the downs can all be used to develop and prepare us for His ultimate plan in our lives. As painful as the events may be, as we pursue Him, He leads the way. As we wrestle with Him, He is patient and gentle. He knows our frame, that we are weak and easily distracted, so He skillfully corrects our course. At last, when we come to the end of our mission and are ushered to our eternal home, we will then clearly see what now seems so hard to discern. Yes, indeed God was masterfully weaving the events of our lives into a marvelous tapestry of eternal value.

Dear Lord, help me to trust you with my life. Help me to surrender my will to yours. Help me to remember that you are in control no matter what I am facing. Keep me O Lord in the center of your will. When I am doubting and confused, veering off course, redirect my steps. I need you to guide me. Thank you for always keeping watch. I look forward to that day when I will finally see you face to face.

AAR Reflections:

1. Are you ready to let God plan your steps? What do you need to let go?

2. Reflect on ways you have seen God redirect your life?

Chapter 9

"Battle Tested"

It was March of 2012 on the first day of spring when my family and I returned from Italy to my hometown. I was very excited to be returning to my home church and was looking forward to seeing all the friends we had left. It was a tiring but joyous day. I was convinced that my stay at the parsonage and my service at the church would lead me into a fulltime ministry position and all would be well. While I was aware that the church was going through some refining, I was confident that I was up for the mission. God had led me back there for a reason and I knew I was called to preach, so in my mind the time had come and God was opening the door.

Part of the agreement for my family and I staying at the parsonage was that I would have to use my GI Bill to attend Bible College and serve in the church in whatever capacity they needed. These are things I planned on doing anyway, so I felt it would be easy for me to live up to my part of the deal, and I was sure I was going to be used in a mighty way. After all, I had put my time in and served God on the front lines of Afghanistan and at our outpost in Italy. I wish I could complete this story with the words "And they lived happily ever after," but this was not to be the case. I do not say that to imply there was or will be a sad ending to the upcoming struggles because ultimately God again used the struggles I would face to draw me closer to Him, and it would be for His honor and Glory. God had been preparing me alright, just not for what I had expected or planned for.

On our first day back, we were greeted by one of the deacons who gave us a key to the house. This would mark the beginning of God showing me the difference between being on the front lines of Afghanistan and being on the front lines of ministry. My family and I realized quickly that the church was going through a major refining period and we ended up right in the middle of it. Division, strife, frustration, and relationship breakdowns were prevalent during this period of time. I will not go into many details because ultimately God had His plan for our lives and His church. God would prepare my family and me for the work He had for us to do there. Even though the pain of seeing and even losing some relationships due to the turmoil the church was experiencing made it difficult, God would use this situation to also refine and use me for His intended purpose. I knew from my past experiences that while the refining process is painful, it is also necessary for growth. God uses these seasons to accomplish, through us as individuals and our churches, the mission and plan He has to further the Gospel. He not only "Battle Tests" individuals, he "Battle Tests" churches to draw them into a deeper level of reliance on Him and to keep us mission focused.

I think it's important to explain the term and title of this chapter for you the reader. God had been working on me very hard during my time in the military, and He used not only the physical struggles but my spiritual struggles so that I would be prepared and "Battle Tested." These struggles strengthened my faith and my ability to persevere and remain mission focused regardless of the challenges I was facing. These lessons were vital, and my experiences would play an important part in the upcoming mission I was called to.

I used the term "Battle tested" in October of 2014, just over two years after my return to New Jersey and to my home church. I was sitting in an interview with a Law Enforcement Agency. For anyone who has tried or gotten a job in law enforcement, you know how tedious and grueling the process is and even making it to the interview stage was an accomplishment. As I sat there for my interview at a large wooden conference table I was grilled with questions from the Undersheriff, Captains, Detectives and other officers. To say I was intimidated would be an understatement.

They questioned me on every mistake and failure I ever made. I can attest I had few, especially being 43 years old at the time of the interview. I can tell you from personal experience, they left no stone unturned from my 43 years on this planet. I remember one question that was directed towards my business failure and bankruptcy. They asked, "How is it that you think you are capable of being a good officer when you have had a business fail and filed for bankruptcy in the last few years?"

I thought about the question for a minute and answered, "I understand your question and even why you are concerned. If I may, I would like to perhaps share with you what I learned from those failures or better put, obstacles. It would be easy for me if I walked in here today with a shining past with no glaring failures, however, I do not see them that way."

They all seemed to perk up in their chairs when I said that. I continued, "I have found that through the toughest times in my life I have continued to move forward regardless of the circumstances. It's really not a question of my mistakes or failures but a question of what I learned and what I did after those events. So, to answer your question. Many may look and see failure and poor decisions. When I look, I see that I have been Battle Tested and continued to push forward and accomplished the mission in spite of my mistakes."

They followed up with many more questions. I must have used the term "Battle Tested" at least five times. I used the term so often that at one point one of the detectives actually asked a question and answered it for me and said, "I guess that means you were Battle Tested" and smiled. I ended up getting the job a few weeks later and one of the Detectives at the interview calls me "Battle Tested" to this day.

I thought it was important for you as the reader to understand that God had changed my perspective on things and I was by His Grace, "Battle Tested," which was the preparation I needed to be effective for His work on the front lines of ministry. It is also important to say that while I had planned on ministry as my vocation, God was answering my desire to be in Law enforcement, which wanted to do since my early twenties. We serve an awesome God, and like any good father, He at times gives us our desires and uses them to achieve His purpose for our life. I was truly blessed to become a Sheriff's Deputy and now have the honor to serve the community I live in.

Trying to integrate back into civilian life was difficult enough, never mind having to deal with the unexpected curveballs that followed my return. The church asked me if I would work with the teens and teach Sunday School for them. I was excited and gladly accepted the new position. I had taught most of these kids in Junior High Sunday school before I left for the military, so it seemed like an easy transition.

Over time I noted that the transition was not going as smoothly as I thought it would. The current struggles at the church had affected not only the adults but the teens as well. At times I was met with unexpected resistance from the teens and even some parents. What I quickly realized is that disjointed relationships and division do not remain isolated, they spread throughout and can cause discouragement and disengagement.

Due to these situations I allowed Satan to plant seeds of bitterness in my heart, and in time I would allow these seeds to be watered. However, I was also more determined than ever to push through because I knew God had a plan for me there. I was after all, "Battle Tested," and quite honestly the more pushback I got the more I felt God was going to use me. In the infantry we are trained to eliminate the closest threat. If you are going to fire on a target, you don't fire on one that's 400 meters away, you fire on the one 50 meters away. Why? Because that is your biggest threat. I say this because Satan does the same thing. He does not waste a lot of time with Christians who are ineffective and not pushing forward. Why? Because that's not his biggest threat. Satan steps up his attacks when Christians begin to move forward with the plan God has for them. So, the more pushback I got from people and circumstances, the more I knew I was headed in the right direction and moving towards God's plan.

I began leading the youth ministry and teaching our teens every Sunday during the second hour after the service. While it was not where I expected to be, it was where God wanted me to be. My teaching style had changed since returning from the military. I no longer looked at our teens as merely kids, but as young adults that God wanted to serve Him in one way or another. I saw two types of people, those who wanted to join the mission God assigned them and those who did not. Now don't get me wrong, I am not saying that people who are not engaged are not in Christ. But I did and do think it was important to encourage those who were not to get engaged with whatever they feel God wants them to do. It was my job as the Youth Minister to teach them scripture and provide opportunities for them to serve under my mentorship.

As I began serving our youth, I started to create opportunities for our teens to engage. We began going to an Inner City Ministry for children once a month and led games, worship, bible teaching, and helped feed the children. We also performed a skit for one of our church events. I tried to get the teens further involved in the life of the church any way I could, set up, clean up, and whatever other needs they could help with at the church. I had bible studies at our home and we shared meals together as often as possible.

The goal was to build unity and rally around whatever mission God put before us. I hung up an idea board, and if any teen had an idea no matter how silly it seemed I would write it down. Then we would spend time during Sunday school running through the ideas and start planning the one the teens seemed most interested in. This started getting the teens unified and engaged in serving God. I felt the ministry was moving along nicely, even though I was still being met with some headwinds from some of the parents and circumstances the church was dealing with at that time.

Of course, "My" plan was to quadruple the size of the youth ministry, and once the pastors and parents saw what God was doing through me, I would surely be asked to come on staff as an Assistant Pastor. Remember the trash can of my plans I spoke about previously. Well, God tossed another one of "my" great plans in that can and I am thankful He did. My track record of trying to intervene in God's timing or plans was poor, to put it mildly.

A few months into the youth ministry, it was decided by the youth and myself that we would start a Youth Group on Sunday Nights to fellowship and share the Love of Christ with all who attended. We all thought this was a great idea. I began giving the teens projects to work on. I wanted them to take ownership of the youth group and use it as a tool to get them engaged in serving God.

All the plans were set, and we scheduled our first meeting to be held at 7 pm on Sunday Nights twice a month. Our first youth group would consist of pizza and painting the youth room. I was encouraged that they all took part in planning this event. I was also encouraged by their enthusiasm and effort in the planning. I treated each event like a military mission and as we planned, I would use what I learned from the military to help them remain mission focused and have a backup plan if needed.

The morning we were supposed to have our first youth group, a man came up to me and said," There are three teenagers from the low-income development next door wondering if they could get some school supplies. Can you talk to them?" I went upstairs and told the kids we did not have any school supplies on hand, but if they came back later to our youth group, I would get some supplies for them then. I was so excited! What an opportunity to serve the community. After the service I told my wife what happened and we gathered up a bunch of school supplies and prepared for our first Youth Group night. God was on the move, leaving us amazed at His faithfulness.

It was 6:30 that night when one of our youth showed up early, excited about the newly established event. I explained to her what happened at church with the three kids from the community. I told her they most likely would not come back, but I was thrilled that they showed up asking for help. I felt God had His hand on this new adventure.

I opened the doors of the church at 6:45 pm and anxiously awaited the arrival of the other youth from our church. As 7 pm rolled around, I explained to the girl who showed up early that it was important not to get discouraged, God would bring the youth and supply the workers. I remember her words to me. "Mr. Lee, how are we going to paint the youth room if no one shows up?" I smiled and said, "God will provide the workers, don't worry."

Now just because I said that does not mean I was convinced myself. I remember thinking to myself, "I guess this room is not getting painted tonight." Of course I did not let her know that. Honestly, I was a little discouraged no one showed up. Then it happened!

As we both looked out the doors we saw a large group of teens walking into the parking lot and towards the doors. It was the three teens from the service that morning and they brought about 15 of their friends. I looked at the girl standing next to me and said, "I told you God would provide workers, I did not say who."

I was just as amazed as she was, but I was not going to let her know that. That was the beginning of what would be a little over a year of ministry to the kids from that neighboring community. God was showing me again it was not going to be on my terms or my way, but on His terms and His way.

God's plan and mission was to use our youth group to reach the youth of that community for as long as He saw fit and to plant the seeds of the Gospel in their hearts. Three of those teens received Christ over that year, and at least 30 to 40 heard the Gospel twice every month. God was unfolding His plan and I was honored to be used by Him for as long as He saw fit.

After about 18 months of serving as the youth minister, my wife and I decided it was time to step aside and handed the ministry over to the Jr. High youth leader. It was hard to give it up, but through prayer I knew it was time. God again was teaching me that when it's time to let something go, He will let you know and if we cling to it beyond His appointed time for us, it's nothing more than pride and not God. I can happily say I learned this lesson, and when I stepped down I felt at peace about it. I strapped myself up with "the Armor of God" and went into the Battle, and through God's strength and His will, fruit was produced despite the pushback from some of the situations around me. I still thank God to this day that He allowed me to minister to those kids. I often see them around town and I know the seeds that were planted will grow in God's time.

I was still fulfilling the agreement I had with the church and studying Biblical Psychology at a local Christian College. I was also working full-time trying to support my family and get back on my feet. It was starting to become clear that my dream and plan of being hired as a full-time pastor was not going to happen. I was disappointed and hurt. It is at this point that I subtly began watering the seeds of bitterness in my heart and they were starting not only to take root, but to sprout.

After stepping down from the youth ministry I began leading a Bible study at the church on Wednesday Nights and ministering to a few guys one-on-one, but lurking under my perseverance and service was a heart that was becoming ensnared with bitterness.

When we are in Christ, we are His and our soul belongs to Him. While Satan cannot have our souls, he can steal our time and attention if we let him. When allowed, he can render us ineffective. I was struggling more and more with some of the discord that was going on at the church and the fact that things were not going as I planned. I wanted to leave the church so bad, but I couldn't because I had no way of supporting my family while attending school full-time and working full-time at a low paying job. God had locked my "escape hatch" and He was not allowing me to leave until my work and His work was done.

Often as Christians, when turmoil hits a church we all too often leave and move on to a church that is more comfortable. The problem with this is that we miss out on God's refining process. We never gain the experience of being "Battle Tested." All too often, we place our own comfort before God's plan and will.

It's amazing how God used my military experiences during this period of my life. I remembered back to those long road marches when I was so tired and could not feel my feet, but I kept moving forward because I did not want to be the soldier that quit and jeopardized the mission.

My answer did not lie in leaving the church and finding a more comfortable situation, it lied in seeing the mission through, regardless of what it cost. After all, compared to what Christ endured for me at the Cross, who was I to complain.

I did, on a few occasions, confront some of the situations that were frustrating me and disappointing me. Looking back, it was really just superficial and not heartfelt, nor could it be since the bitterness had taken hold at this point.

My heart was becoming more and more consumed by bitterness and my intention of addressing these situations was not to restore a relationship or solve a problem, but to let them know how hurt I was. I was like a kid in a candy store crying and screaming because I was not allowed to get what I wanted. I wanted people to see I was justified in the way I felt and to say that

I was right, so I could move on and satisfy my desire to win the battle and feed my pride, which was what fueled my bitterness.

Instead, God was trying to teach me that true forgiveness and restoration was not contingent on a response, but on my heart. My battle was not with others or the situation at the church but with my sin of bitterness and pride that I allowed to grow in my heart subtly since I returned.

God was also teaching me that I was incapable of forgiving without true repentance. I lacked the understanding that I could only forgive when I understood that my sin was the issue not someone else's. I needed to repent and remember what Christ had forgiven me of.

My heart remained in a bitter state for quite some time, even while I still served and continued to attend school. When the bitterness was fully grown I was rendered ineffective and lacked the power I needed from the Holy Spirit to move ahead with the mission. My mission, without realizing it, became a desire to be justified in my bitterness rather than to follow God's plan and to trust Him.

I remember one day, Pastor Mike Tapia asked me after a Sunday Service if I would like to help teach Community Group time. I think my response surprised him. I flat out said "No! I was not interested in teaching or being in any part of leading anything."

I am sure I gave him a host of reasons, but the bottom line was that I was consumed with bitterness. I did not know it at the time, but God would use this man to speak truth into my life and soften my heart.

I thank God for the trials I experienced before coming back to my home church because without those trials I would not have been "Battle Tested' and would have likely succumbed to the trials God had laid at my feet. It was through the God-given perseverance, faith, and the intervention of others that God would begin to soften my heart and untangle the web of bitterness and pride which had ensnared me.

In 2 Corinthians 11:24-28 we read, "From the Jews five times I received forty stripes minus one. Three times I was beaten with rods; once I was stoned; three times I was shipwrecked; a night and a day I have been in the deep; in journeys often, in perils of water, in perils of robbers, in perils of my own countrymen, in perils of the Gentiles, in perils in the city, in perils in the wilderness, in perils in the sea, in perils among false brethren; in weariness and toil, in sleeplessness often, in hunger and thirst, in fasting's often, in cold and nakedness, besides the other things, what comes upon me daily: my deep concern for all the churches."

I think it is safe to say that Paul was "Battle Tested." As followers of Christ, hardships and disappointments are part of God's design to conform us into the image of His Son. I once heard it said that "The harsher the wind, the stronger the tree."

Trees that withstand the strong winds have set down deeper roots. The stress of the winds a tree faces while it is growing help it to not only set deeper roots, but also allow its trunk to grow stronger along the lines of stress. God uses circumstances and disappointments in our lives to help us grow deeper roots. In other words, we become "Battle Tested" and better able to serve Him and bring Him Glory. In the same way that God allows the stormy winds to blow on His creation, He allows the storms of life to fashion us into "Battle Tested" servants of the Most High.

Dear Lord, help me to seek you when the stormy winds of life come my way. Use these storms and disappointments in my life to mold me into the person you are calling me to be. Lead me through these storms that I may be better able to fight the good fight of faith. Oh Lord, that I may be Battle Tested for your Glory.

AAR reflection:

1. How have you dealt with the disappointments and trials in your life? Have they caused you to grow deeper roots as you trust in Him, or have you tried to endure them on your own?

2. How does this idea of being "Battle Tested" encourage you to stay the course?

Chapter 10

"Green Light Go!"

I will start this chapter by saying I have been blessed deeply by God through my trials, struggles, bitterness, loss, and grief. God saw fit and still sees fit to invest His grace, love, mercy and patience with me. As I write this final chapter of my personal testimony, it is my hope and prayer that you will find encouragement in knowing that our God is perfectly consistent and persistent when it comes to preparing us for the mission He has for us to accomplish. It is when we submit to His purposes for our lives that we begin to experience true joy and peace.

As I stated in the last chapter, I was ensnared in bitterness fueled by my pride. My problem was not that I knew God had a plan and was preparing me for it, my problem was that I thought I knew where, when, and how His plan "should" be executed in my life. My incessant urge to make it happen my way opened my heart up to bitterness, frustration, and the desire to make my voice heard. Buried beneath my perseverance to get the mission accomplished was a desire to get what I thought I deserved and had earned. This was a recipe for ineffectiveness as the sins of selfish ambition and bitterness guided my actions instead of allowing God to lead me into His purpose in His time.

It was during this period of ineffectiveness and bitterness that God put Pastor Mike in my life. He took me under his wing and began to disciple me. Pastor Mike became my mentor and my friend. He would sit and listen as I spewed out all the injustices that had happened to me.

I would share how I knew God had a plan for me, but people and circumstances kept getting in my way. I shared how I thought God wanted me to be a pastor and serve God on a full-time basis. I shared many of the trials I had experienced and could not understand why I was not getting what I wanted.

How he sat there week after week and listened to all the nonsense I spewed is beyond me, but he did. He would always say simple wise things to me like, "John, you are a leader not because you say you are but because God says you are. You can't run from it. It is just what God designed you to do."

This baffled me because I had no idea what he or God saw in me. I would ask questions like, "If I am a leader, then why am I not a pastor or leading anything?" He would share with me his experiences and often say, "It's in God's time and in His way and not yours."

Week after week we would meet to pray, talk, and study God's Word, and each week I was blown away by the God-given wisdom and guidance I received during our meetings. As time drew on, I began to open up more and more to Pastor Mike about what was going on in my heart and the bitterness I was harboring.

He told me in no uncertain terms that unless I let go of the bitterness I would remain ineffective and would never accomplish what God had for me to accomplish. I told him I tried on several occasions to address my bitterness with the people and the circumstances I thought were causing it. I also explained that no matter how hard I tried, I just could not seem to break the chains.

In time, his words of encouragement and Godly wisdom started to break through. The reality was, that as much as I thought I had been broken by all that I went through, I was still clinging to sin and it was ensnaring me. God needed me broken and contrite, so He could intervene and use me. God was waiting patiently for me to come to that point, and he was placing people and situations in my life to help that process along.

Then it happened at one of our regular meeting nights. I cannot remember what scripture Pastor Mike pointed out to me, but he told me that I needed to repent of my sin first with God and then with the people I held bitterness against. I was confused because I felt like I had searched myself and truly could not see what I had done.

He told me, "Your sin is bitterness and until you repent for that bitterness it will continue to consume you and you will continue to be ineffective in what God has planned for you." It was then, at that moment that my eyes, and more importantly, my heart was opened. I was bitter, and that bitterness was a sin that was distracting me from the mission God had assigned me. I was like that soldier who was constantly complaining, "It's too cold, it's too hard, why should I have to do this," or like that annoying kid in the back seat asking how much farther until he gets there every few minutes. I realized my sin was the obstacle, not the circumstances or people around me.

I went home that night and prayed, and all the faces of the people I was bitter towards came to my mind. I saw how my pride was driving me to pursue my mission not God's. I prayed and asked Christ to forgive me for harboring bitterness in my heart.

I also asked Christ to forgive me for my sin of pride and to search my heart and reveal what other sins I was clinging to. He opened my eyes to the sins I was clinging to and it was then I realized my brokenness and need for Him to be in charge and not me.

The freedom, peace, and joy I felt were indescribable and I knew what I had to do. I had to not only repent to God, but seek out those I was harboring bitterness towards and ask for their forgiveness. This time I would seek nothing from them in return. It was at that point through God that the bitterness vanished and through the power of the Holy Spirit I was able to forgive the people and let go of the circumstances that were weighing me down. In some cases, relationships were restored, in some they were not but truly it did not matter because I was right with God and the bitterness had subsided.

When a Paratrooper is preparing to jump they are given a set of instructions as they approach the drop zone. You stand up, hook up your static line (which is what deploys your parachute), do final checks of your equipment and your buddies equipment, and then wait. It doesn't matter how many jumps you have made, each time the instructions are repeated.

There is a red light, usually by the door. When that light turns green the Jump Master yells "Green Light Go!" Your job at that point is to GO! Depending on the size of the drop zone you have about 20 seconds to get 15 Paratroopers to jump out of that door on each side of the aircraft. I share this because once I repented and God removed the bitterness, I could almost hear the words "Green Light Go!" God wanted me to jump out into His plan and accomplish the mission He had for me.

I was still attending Bible college during this period and my classes were coming to an end. I was in an accelerated program, so I attended class once a week for four hours at a time and the semesters were six weeks long. I cannot remember what class I had, but it was brought to my attention by my doctor that I would need to have my gall bladder removed. This meant I would miss the second week of my new semester class to recover. I met the new professor and pulled him aside. I explained that I would have to miss one week but was willing to make up the work.

His response was not one I expected. He told me that school policy dictated that if I missed a class, I might as well just go home because I needed to attend all the classes to earn the credits. I was extremely unhappy with his response and even more unhappy with what I felt was a lack of grace.

I left class that night pretty upset and thought it was for the best because I would not want to sit through his class anyway. When I got home I explained to my wife what happened, and she simply said, "At least you won't have to deal with him again. You can make up that class later."

After recovering from my surgery I went back to school and started a different class in my Bachelors program. I sat there and waited for the professor to walk in and much to my dismay it was the same professor that taught the class I had to drop. I can tell you I was not very happy, and I was certainly having impure thoughts to say the least.

I endured my time under his teaching for six long weeks. At our last session our assignment was to give a brief testimony about a struggle we had and how God helped us through it. So, I grudgingly stood in front of the class and shared my testimony with the class and the professor.

As God would have it, the professor came up to me after the class and shared with me that He ran a chapel service every Sunday at a Rescue Mission near where I lived. He invited me to pop in one Sunday and share my testimony. He thought it would be good for the men there to hear it. I told him I would think about it, but honestly, I did not care for this guy too much, so I was not planning on going. As I drove home, the thought came to me, "You know what, I am going to show up. I am going to call his bluff." Or so I thought.

I showed up that next Sunday and preached to about 30 homeless men at the Rescue Mission. I fell in love with those guys immediately. The professor came up to me afterwards and asked if I minded running the chapel service once a month, so he could have a break. I agreed and said, "I would be honored."

The professor and I ended up becoming friends. The irony is that God was using this man to fulfill His plan for my life. One Sunday my professor friend told me he was moving and asked if I would mind taking over the Chapel service on Sunday. I was humbled at the opportunity and gladly agreed. The rest is history.

I began preaching every Sunday night at the Rescue Mission and even began bringing some men from my church who wanted to serve. I still lead the Chapel service at the Rescue mission to this day, and I can honestly say there is no other place I would rather preach then to these men. God has used this ministry in a mighty way.

My plan was not to preach at a Rescue Mission to the homeless. I was convinced I would be preaching in a nice cozy church, getting pats on the back for a great message. Looking back, God assigned me His mission not mine and I am honored to be a part of it.

I continued to meet with Pastor Mike, but things were now a bit different. Once the bitterness had vanished, God began to open doors of ministry for me. Pastor Mike and I became more ministry partners and friends and my whining sessions became more of how can we be used by God sessions.

We began to bounce ministry ideas off one another on how we could engage the church, preach the Gospel, and bring the hope of Christ to those around us. We began organizing outreach events at our church in the hopes of bringing the Light of the Gospel to the surrounding communities. After organizing and preaching at several events both big and small, Pastor Mike asked if I would consider leading the Outreach Ministry at our church. I am happy to say I accepted. God has done amazing things through the Outreach ministry and I am honored to be a part of it.

I could write forever about how God's Love, Mercy, and Grace have impacted my life. How He as the Perfect Father continues to refine me and guide me into His plan for my life, but that would be a never ending book. My hope in writing these experiences is to encourage you that indeed God does have a plan for your life. God uses ordinary men like you and me to accomplish His extraordinary plans as we wait on Him and rely on His power. Not only do we not fully know what is good for us, as I have learned, our plans are not His plans. Was I called to preach? Yes, I was called to preach, just not where, when, or how I thought I would.

I had blinders on and God needed to remove them. I thought that because I had the call to preach, that meant I needed to be a pastor at a church and it had to be my vocation. I think many Christians make that assumption and its simply not the case. Our calling has nothing to do with what our worldly vocation is. What God has called us to is not defined by a job description or by our profession, it is simply what He has designed us to do. It's not a vocation it's our purpose, and we are to fulfill that purpose regardless of what our vocation is.

God chose to fulfill my dream of becoming a Law Enforcement Officer at the ripe old age of 43, and yet that did not change the fact that I am called to preach His word. Whether I am a plumber, a pastor, or a paratrooper, I was created to accomplish the work He has for me. Our walk with Christ is not confined or limited by time, it is eternal, beyond time and only limited by our own fears.

I often ask myself, "Who am I that He loves me so much?" I guess we can all ask ourselves that question. Through God, I went from a Paratrooper to a Preacher. You just can't make this stuff up, its truly divine intervention. In closing. I will share a poem that was taken from a dead confederate soldier the author is anonymous:

A Christian Confederate Soldier's Prayer

(Anon - alleged to have been found on a CSA casualty at the
Devil's Den, Gettysburg)

"I asked God for strength, that I might achieve.

I was made weak, that I might learn humbly to obey.

I asked for health, that I might do greater things.

I was given infirmity, that I might do better things.

I asked for riches, that I might be happy.

I was given poverty, that I might be wise.

I asked for power that I might have the praise of men.

I was given weakness, that I might feel the need of God.

I asked for all things, that I might enjoy life.

I was given life, that I might enjoy all things.

I got nothing that I asked for but got everything I had hoped for.

Almost despite myself, my unspoken prayers were answered.

I am, among all people, most richly blessed."

Dear Lord, God almighty, Creator of the heavens and earth, who am I that you are mindful of me. Help me to accept your will in your timing and in your strength. Give me the patience to wait when I am to wait, and the courage to move when I am to move. I thank you that you are patient with me and never give up, even in the face of my impatience. God, you are Sovereign and I commit myself this day to seek you first daily that I would be ready when I hear you whisper, Green light Go."

AAR reflection:

1. Have you ever found yourself with such bitterness that it was robbing you of joy? How did you respond? Did you confess it, or are you still holding onto it?
2. What is God calling you to be part of? How will you respond when you hear the Commander of the Heavenly Host signal, "Green light, Go? Are you ready?

Final After Action Report

Now that you have read this book, what are you prepared to do about it? Remember, this is an after action report and as such it requires you to act. As you reflect on the previous chapters and their respective calls to action, I ask again, what are you prepared to do?

First, if you do not know Jesus Christ as your Lord and Savior, if you have never repented of your sins and asked His forgiveness, then your action and mission is clear. "Submit to His Lordship," turn from your sins and receive His grace and mercy.

John 3:16-17 says, "For God so loved the world that He gave His only begotten Son, that whosoever believes in Him should not perish but have everlasting life. For God did not send His Son into the world to condemn the world but that the world through Him might be saved."

You see, without Christ we all stand condemned because of our sin, "He who believes in the Son has everlasting life; and he who does not believe the Son shall not see life, but the wrath of God abides on him", (John 3:36). In Christ's death, God demonstrated His love towards us, in that while we were still sinners, He who was without sin, gave Himself in exchange for us.

There is no other way. In John 14:6, Jesus said, "I am the way, the truth and the life, No one comes to the Father except through Me."

If you do not know Christ as your personal Savior, as I said before, your mission is clear, repent and receive His forgiveness today while you still can. If you are ready to act, then say this prayer:

Dear God in Heaven, I know that I am a sinner. I realize that there is nothing that I can do to deserve your favor. I believe you sent your Son Jesus to die on the cross for my sins, and now the best way I know how, I am asking you to forgive my sins once and for all, save my soul and give me the free gift of eternal life. From this day forward, I want to live my life for you. Thank you for hearing my prayer. Amen.

If you have prayed this prayer for the first time, we would love to hear from you and send you something to help you grow in your new life with Christ. Just email us at:

paratrooper2preacher@gmail.com

Secondly, if you are already a Christian, I believe your mission is just as clear, Take up your cross and follow Him.

"Then Jesus said to His disciples, "If anyone desires to come after Me, let him deny himself, and take up his cross, and follow me. For whoever desires to save his life will lose it, but whoever loses his life for My sake will find it." (Matthew 16:24-25)

Remember, the cross was a symbol of great suffering and death. Jesus was telling His disciples that in order to follow Him, they would need to deny themselves and take up their cross. Now, this does not sound like a call to ease and comfort, but a call to great sacrifice. Sacrifice, yes, but no greater than the sacrifice our dear Savior paid for us.

Christ calls us to action, we are in a battle for the souls of men. God uses ordinary people to be part of His extraordinary plan. Will you answer the call?

About the Authors

John Lee is an ex US Army Paratrooper. He served in Afghanistan with the 173rd airborne combat team. He is married with three children and currently serves as a Sheriff's Officer. In addition, he is the outreach coordinator at his local church and serves as a chapel leader to a community rescue mission. He studied Biblical Psychology at Pillar College in Zarephath, New Jersey.

Dr. Mike Tapia is an American Pastor and School administrator currently serving in New Jersey. He is married and has four children. He holds a master's degree in Theological Studies from Southwestern Baptist Theological Seminary. In addition, he has earned a bachelor's degree in Biological Science and is a retired Chiropractic Physician.

80738167R00075

Made in the USA
Middletown, DE
17 July 2018